AND BREATHE...

PREVENT, MANAGE AND MASTER DIFFICULT LEADERSHIP CONVERSATIONS IN BUSINESS AND BEYOND!

NICOLE POSNER

Disclaimer

In parts throughout this book, the author has described events, locales and conversations from their memories. Sometimes, in order to maintain their anonymity in some instances, they have changed the names of individuals and places, they may have changed some identifying characteristics and details such as physical properties, occupations and places of residence.

Copyright © 2022 by Nicole Posner

ISBN13 Paperback: 978-1-913728-91-5

ISBN13 Hardback: 978-1-913728-92-2

All rights reserved.

No part of this book may be reproduced in any form or by any electronic or mechanical means, including information storage and retrieval systems, without written permission from the author, except for the use of brief quotations in a book review.

CONTENTS

Foreword	5
Introduction	7
PART I **PREVENTION**	
1. Understanding Difficult Conversations	17
2. Awareness	28
3. Communication	43
4. The Three Archetypes	59
5. Assumptions and Expectations	74
PART II **CURE**	
6. It all starts with you!	91
7. Tools, Tips and Techniques	109
8. Communication Rules	130
9. Feedback and Recognition	150
10. Managing The Conversations	168
Epilogue	204
About the Author	205

FOREWORD

As a family divorce lawyer for over 40 years and a Partner at Mishcon de Reya, I have seen firsthand the damage from broken relationships and the chaos created through unresolved conflict and poor communication.

In my experience, these same behaviours apply in a business context. Many toxic situations could have been avoided in the workplace by engaging in honest and transparent conversations as well as enlisting supportive guidance to navigate difficult dialogues with better judgement and skill. All of which create a business culture where employees can thrive stimulating productivity and growth.

I have known Nicole for nearly 20 years and have spent countless hours discussing conflict and communication with her, listening to her wisdom around challenging people dynamics as she demonstrated effective methods to address them.

Her practical advice, knowledge and thought provoking conversations have always impressed me and left me with no doubt why she is best placed to write this book.

It is packed full of examples and lightbulb moments that resonate with everyday challenges in business and the workplace. She illustrates how easy it is to get it wrong and offers an abundance of tools to get it right.

I was gripped from the first page as her writing style is conversational and so easy to assimilate as she shares insights which seem obvious but so definitely are not for those who have limited experience in managing people.

I really enjoyed the helpful way she organises the book into problems, her analysis of them followed by sensible solutions allowing the reader to dip in and out.

In my view everyone can draw some golden nuggets from this book and learn to navigate communication better as the easily digestible acronyms, tools and techniques also have a wider application for almost any difficult conversation beyond the workplace.

I believe all organisations could improve the way in which they manage their people. This book is an invaluable guide to support them to do so. It can only be a win / win to provide their leaders with a copy of it!

A very helpful and unmissable guide for any leader or business owner!

Sandra Davis,
Partner, Mishcon de Reya

INTRODUCTION

Sitting on the floor of a small back office on a crisp November morning, I wondered what on earth I was doing.

This was my first ever mediation.

The sun was streaming through dusty windows yet the atmosphere in the room was anything but bright. Next to me, huddled in the corner against a metal cupboard was a middle-aged lady, sobbing into her handkerchief. She was desperate, broken and clearly in need of more support than just the mediation.

While I sat quietly listening to her through muffled tears, I reflected on why this situation had ever reached this tragic and desperate stage and how it had escalated to the point that she and I were sharing this intimate and painful moment.

It only took a few more mediations for me to understand the bigger picture.

My discussions with her manager and many other leaders and business owners along my journey highlighted one glaring and common thread. Genuine confusion. They had no idea what to say for the best in those moments when they felt out of their depth. No clue how to even begin some of those uncomfortable dialogues. No knowledge or experience how to lower the tension in prickly interactions. No certainty that what they did say would be received well or heard at all.

The outcome was either avoidance or a stream of mismanaged situations that instead of being curtailed or nipped in the bud, spiralled quickly out of control.

The fall out and impact of both actions was far reaching. It was destructive to not just relationships but also to the business and the emotional well-being of those within it.

It may come as no surprise that these issues don't disappear or resolve themselves without intervention... as easy and wonderful as that would be!

Which means they simply fester or manifest into a crisis becoming far more complex and time consuming to address at a later date.

It may require a tough conversation with teams around poor performance, attitude, unacceptable behaviour or unwelcome feedback. It might mean facing strong personalities who favour resistance over acceptance. It can lead to uncomfortable discussions around an employee's emotional health, managing a clash with a colleague or playing moderator between two feisty team members. It might require skilful and delicate navigation around boundaries with clients who take advantage of your good nature or employees who were once your colleagues. And as for tricky conversations around client payments... just the thought of it can trigger a wave of nausea!

And what about you?

The impending conversation can play out in your head repeatedly. And then comes the churn, especially if you anticipate it might not end well. Will you experience pushback? Will you manage it confidently or will you bumble your way through it? Will you lose your focus and become derailed? Will you hit a wall of silence or a brick wall?

And what are the consequences for you personally if it all goes pear shaped?

Your reputation and trust as an effective leader, manager or business owner might be under scrutiny. You may lose confidence in your own abilities to lead. You may be faced with more time-consuming issues to address that have since materialised out of the original issues. Your relationships with colleagues and clients might suffer causing irreparable damage. You might carry the weight of this burden with you into your home life placing stress on your personal relationships with friends and family. You may experience sleepless nights wracked with worry and fear affecting your own mental health and emotional wellbeing.

And as for the business ...

Poor behaviours will invariably continue which also sends a clear message to others... that toxic communication is ok. The fall out damaging relationships with other colleagues as well as hindering projects and collaborations. Morale and performance might take a nosedive. Productivity slumps. Confusion in communication leads to missed deadlines and targets, unhappy clients, and an increase in sick related absence. Mounting pressure on the rest of the business creates disruption and resentment as colleagues are forced to pick up slack. Valued employees join *The Great Resignation*. Clients take their business elsewhere following disruptive management of their account as key members of their team move on. While you take your eye off the ball continuously fighting fires and spending less time on client relationships and running the business.

None of which is good!

But imagine if you had the secret to effortlessly prevent any of this manifesting? Instead becoming empowered to lean into these conversations with confidence and achieve successful outcomes time and again. To have a host of tools, techniques, and strategies at your fingertips to support and guide you to have these crucial discussions without feeling overwhelmed, frustrated, worried or afraid. To manage awkward situations with a little more tact and less tenacity. To overcome your fears, phobias, challenges, and blocks. To breeze through any challenging conversation with ease. To lead your teams and serve your clients without that onerous black cloud hovering overhead. To build strong relationships so you build bridges, not burn them. To have a business that runs like clockwork because the atmosphere and culture is a happy, harmonious, and collaborative one. Wouldn't that be nice?

So why me?

My communication journey began as a *Workplace Mediator*. My training was underpinned with insights into the psychology of conflict. I learned why we are triggered, why we see the red mist that sparks a fiery response. I understood why we dig our heels in and become entrenched in our beliefs and why we remain stuck and can't find a way forward.

Having studied psychology as a hobby for six years prior, people and their behaviours have always fascinated me but so has the way we communicate. I have no doubt this stemmed from my early career in PR and Communications.

I spent many years mediating crisis after crisis, although at times challenging, it was proved to be enlightening. I unravelled misunderstandings, explored unmet needs of those in conflict, encouraged them to view their unique situation through a different lens and to imagine how great tomorrow would be if they could work through their differences. I guided them to find solutions that worked for everyone. But the essence behind all this was how to communicate in a healthier and more effective way in the future. And how to have difficult conversations in the first place to prevent the need for interventions at all.

What I took from every situation was that parties in the mediation were often left wondering 'now what?'. They were unsure what to do with all the information they learnt about themselves during the process. And the leaders and business owners knew they were often at the heart of everyone's troubles but at a loss how to manage the conversations better. I realized I could support them through coaching which is why I extended my credentials to become an accredited Executive Communication and Conflict Coach and why I now also train leaders and consult for businesses to help them craft a culture of respectful, open, and honest communication.

My hope is that this book will support you to feel empowered and confident to iron out bumps in relationships before they become molehills. I hope that you learn how to manage difficult conversations effortlessly and courageously so that your department or businesses will run smoothly allowing you the time and focus to direct your attention on your vision and goals. And more importantly I hope that you sleep soundly in the knowledge that the conversation went well, and you experience that exquisite relief that it's over. *And Breathe...*

Many of my clients have expressed those lightbulb moments after working with me when the penny finally drops and they can finally see that beacon of light directing them through their difficulties. They are able to view their situation through a different lens and acknowledge the conversations don't have to be so challenging to manage once they know how. They can see the difference it brings to relationships and team dynamics, performance and productivity and the status quo. Fear, negativity, and ill feeling are quashed and replaced with positive energy. The equilibrium is rebalanced so the workplace and business can thrive once again.

They have understanding, perspective, a clear framework and logical steps to move difficult conversations forward rather than communicating from a place of fear, confusion, and a scattergun approach. They don't need to hide behind meetings and excuses.

This is what you will discover as you turn the pages.

'And Breathe...' is split into two parts: Prevention and Cure.

Part One focuses on 'Conflict Prevention' and will demystify the myths behind difficult conversations. It explains the psychology and fear which steers you away from stepping in and leads you into trouble! It allows you to understand communication and your own personal style and triggers which impacts how you show up. It unravels why conversations go wrong or there is a need for them in the first place.

Part Two focuses on 'Conflict Cure' sharing mindset tools to support you to prepare for every challenging interaction, an armoury of effective and practical tips, techniques, anecdotes, and strategies to approach each situation with confidence, courage, compassion, and consideration without ruffling feathers or rocking the status quo enabling you to focus on the business of business.

We will look at the importance of listening, empathy, curiosity, and preparation and focus on a host of conversations that can feel challenging. This includes conversations such as managing attitude, apathy, behaviours, and performance issues, delivering tough feedback, confrontational conversations with colleagues or business partners, awkward conversations with clients and uncomfortable conversations around personal issues and mental health.

You can either dip in and out of the book to the relevant chapters or read it from cover to cover. Whatever you wish.

Whether you are a business owner, leader, HR director, consultant or entrepreneur thinking about expanding your empire, there will plenty of valuable nuggets throughout the book to help you explore why conversations backfire and relationships breakdown and then how to salvage them and restore the equilibrium for a calmer, more dynamic, industrious, and happy workplace.

My hope is that you will be equipped with everything you need to work through your challenging conversations without fear or uncertainty but instead with knowledge, confidence, and skill so that you breeze through them effortlessly, relieved that it wasn't so hard after all! *And Breathe...*

PART I
PREVENTION

"If we understand what creates and drives conflict, we can minimise the need for the difficult conversations in the first place".

— *NICOLE POSNER*

1

UNDERSTANDING DIFFICULT CONVERSATIONS

> "Difficult conversations are almost never about getting the facts right. They are about conflicting perceptions, interpretations and values."
>
> — DOUGLAS STONE

To prevent conflict, we need to not only understand what fuels it but how to communicate through it. Let's look at what sits behind those difficult conversations in order to navigate them more efficiently.

I've never met a person who hasn't, at some point in their life, faced a difficult conversation in their personal or business life. Even if you are blessed with the most passive and *Zen* disposition, there will always be a situation that you come across that feels uncomfortable to navigate.

So, let's start with an obvious question... what is a difficult conversation?

It's an important conversation that really matters. If it wasn't, let's be honest, we wouldn't really care about it! It's a challenging one that has the potential to ruffle feathers. One that makes your stomach churn, and you dread. One where the stakes are high, and you worry how it will play out and the consequences if it doesn't go to plan. One you might fear or chose to avoid but know you can't. One you ruminate over until the early hours of the morning. One that feels as if there is so much resting on the outcome.

And if we don't like having them, there's a high probability we will try to avoid them altogether. We will kick the can down the road or put them off for another day and then another.

Whatever is at the core, that conversation can go two ways. If you procrastinate or mismanage it, the chances are the problem will escalate. If successful, agreements and decisions will be made effortlessly and without conflict. And relationships with your teams, clients, business partners and colleagues will flourish and thrive.

Yet if we can uncover our resistance, we can address it and move forward. Because avoidance should never be a choice action.

In my experience there are four reasons we dodge these conversations: Fear, Limiting Beliefs, Lack of Skill or Time Constraints.

Fear

In most cases it is the anticipation of the conversation that invokes anxiety, concern, pain and fear. Past experiences of challenging situations are powerful reminders that trigger our 'Fight, Flight or Freeze' response warning us that the same catastrophe is sure to re-occur. So, we become nervous as we relive that moment of anger or trepidation.

Perhaps that fear takes you back to a previous occasion where you faced pushback or confrontation, or it revives memories where you lost control of the conversation. Maybe it reminds you of a time where you appeared incompetent in front of your peers or teams, failing to convince stakeholders to invest in your ideas, looking inept or foolish when the stakes were high. And that's not a feeling you relish or want to experience again.

Or it could be a fear of conflict itself which you are programmed to walk away from. Perhaps your star performer is a bully and you prefer not to rock the boat by confronting their behaviour as it could impact revenue or monthly targets, let alone team dynamics.

And in the same vein, what about if that difficult conversation is with one of your business partners or colleagues who brings in all the bucks but terrorizes your teams. The problem goes deeper because you are afraid to stand up to them so remain silent and unsupportive of your teams who chose to vote with their feet… and walk to join *The Great Resignation*.

Maybe the culture is *'put up and shut up'* so the fear to speak up outweighs the benefits of having the conversation because it feels like there is no buffer or safety support mechanism in place to share your opinions. And what about your reputation? You might experience a stabbing fear of judgement, shame and humiliation of being perceived as an ineffective weak leader if you don't manage the conversation competently.

Lack of Skills

Skill set, or a lack of it, inhibits many new leaders and managers. There is often an expectation that they *should* know what to say or how to address a situation. Yet without proper support or training, they don't feel adequately equipped to step in and step up when they need to. A leadership role is unique in so much as it's effectively a brand-new job to the one that a freshly promoted manager may have been performing extremely well in before. Yet new managers are often thrown in the proverbial *Lion's Den* and left unsupported to sink or swim. And that's often when mistakes can happen.

Equally, you might be a new business owner or entrepreneur who has never managed a team before. As your business evolves and grows and you recruit employees (perhaps for the first time), unless you invest in personal development, those skills will be scarce. The confidence and expertise to manage those difficult conversations will be lacking and when problems emerge, the default might be avoidance.

Conversely, I have come across experienced leaders or business owners who have been running the show for a while yet never acquired the appropriate people management skills and think it's too late... so why bother now? They are so set in their ways and long in the tooth, they believe it's often easier to plod along putting out fires and skirting around issues rather than upskilling and learning to address the conversations head on.

But there's more. It might simply boil down to your nature. If you are someone who becomes easily flustered or lack the eloquence of your conversational partner, that lack of verbal skills will impede your management of the conversation so you might decide better to leave it well alone than make a hash of it.

And then there are those emotive and compassionate conversations. The ones where your teams share personal struggles affecting their mental health or situations where you need to impart unpopular and unwelcome news. These conversations are uncomfortable. Unless you have the right tools in your tools box to manage these issues sensitively and empathetically, they are often brushed under the carpet for as long as possible to protect you all from the awkwardness of a public display of emotions.

Limiting Beliefs

Limiting Beliefs can be very constricting. They can stop us in our tracks and prevent us from taking action. And they come in many guises. Some of the avoidance tactics I have encountered over the years have been based on the following beliefs:

- The situation will surely settle down on its own so there's no point in getting involved.
- It's a waste of time because those involved never listen so why would they now?
- You haven't had much success in the past so what's the point of another ineffective attempt at it.
- You will probably escalate the issue because people management skills aren't your greatest strengths.
- At your stage of your career, you should be able to manage these conversations well so it's embarrassing that you don't. You will be judged by your teams, your boss, your colleagues and your clients for your hopeless attempt at people management and your

reputation as an ineffective leader will be cast in stone forevermore!
- Your relationships will be damaged beyond repair if you can't fix issues.

Time Constraints

Another familiar excuse I hear around avoidance is: *'I don't have the time to deal with this now'*. And that's fair enough as long as *now* doesn't stretch out to next week or next month or the one after. In my experience this is often a ruse to sidestep the difficult conversation and more often than not, if it is left, that conversation will be much stickier to manage in a week, two weeks or longer, and ironically so much more time consuming (and often costly) to address at a later date.

The Cost of Avoidance

This might be an opportune time to discuss the cost of avoidance in a little more detail. I recently read a fascinating book by Organisational Psychologist Liane Davey entitled 'The Good Fight'. In it, she explains a great concept called 'conflict debt'.

Like financial debt that incurs interest if the debt isn't repaid immediately, conflict debt has many consequences too.

Liane explains that the longer you leave an unresolved conflict, the more entrenched and problematic it becomes and the deeper it sits until after some time, it feels too hard and difficult to manage at all. You don't know where to even begin and often so many other problems have stacked on top of the original issues, you might have lost sight of what it was that triggered the situation at the start. You seem to be stuck in a black hole with no way out.

The tension mounts, pressure builds, the atmosphere becomes uncomfortable for everyone, and nothing ever changes. That's not just frustrating, it's a very unhelpful and unhealthy way to operate and run a department or business. As you might expect, that's when your relationships will really suffer with colleagues, business partners and clients and the knock-on effect to the rest of your teams and business in general is far reaching.

As we all know, every action has a consequence and avoidance (which is ironically also an action) is no different.

The group mediation I referred to in the introductory chapter is a perfect example of how avoidance can escalate a problem into a crisis.

Several days prior, I had a call with the manager who had requested the mediation. With the very best intentions, she had tried everything in her *own limited* toolbox to move the situation forward.

As she briefed me, I began to get a sense of why my services were requested. It was complicated, but it hadn't started that way. And that was the key.

It appeared to be a case of *'he said, she said'*, followed by denials, accusations, and misunderstandings mixed with high emotion and tears.

I'm not going to lie.... It was messy!

I could understand why the manager had felt ill equipped to resolve the twists and turns as the drama played out however in my opinion her biggest mistake, was to paper over the cracks, rather than address the cause.

She created a schedule for a kitchen rota to ensure none of the group bumped into each other during the working day and arranged for all their desks to face outwards so they had limited opportunity to see or talk to each other or create any further discord and chaos.

This is avoidance at its most unhelpful; you can begin to understand why their differences reached crisis point.

Houston… We have a problem…

Another reason why difficult conversations are often side-stepped is because some managers or business owners are blissfully unaware that there is a problem brewing or haven't acknowledged the severity of it. Perhaps that's inexperience or a choice to ignore the signs but either way, if you're not tuned into potential hotspots surfacing, you can't manage them until it's often progressed too far.

I will cover 'behaviours' in more detail in the following chapters but a point to note is never to take unusual behaviours at face value. What do I mean by that? A behaviour that is out of the ordinary is always a symptom of something else so if a colleague, team member or business partner is 'acting up', that usually indicates *something is up*!

Signs to look out for might include a bubbly team member who becomes unusually quiet. If you ask if they are ok and they answer 'fine', let me assure you nine times out of ten, that means they are not, so this would be the time to gently probe a little deeper.

Changes in routine and attitude are a key indicator that all is not well. Employees who sign in late or stroll into the office with less gusto is an early warning flag to take note of. As are snappy responses or equally no response and a general air of apathy. Obsessive complaints, niggles and skirmishes with business partners and resistance to new ideas all create an environment where negativity and toxic behaviours easily spread and impact the workplace and general status quo.

And this outcome is the *only* one you want to avoid... not all the warning beacons that indicate there is trouble on the horizon and a difficult conversation looming.

Why Does It Go Wrong Before It's Begun?

If you've taken the first step to initiate the conversation, you're one step closer to moving the needle. However, you want to ensure it goes to plan but in order to do that, you need to understand why a conversation can turn on its head at the drop of a hat or even in some cases, before it begins.

There are many factors that contribute to the success or failure of a challenging conversation. So, let's start with your positioning of it. Even the language you use to arrange the conversation can impact how it pans out.

For example, if you request a meeting with a colleague or team member with the subject heading '*We need to talk*', that might provoke a range of responses. Some prickly. Some nervous. Some angry. Some confused. Some fearful.

While you might be rushing out to a meeting and quickly tapping out the email with no ill intention, others won't know that. And so, before the conversation has even begun, you might have paved the way for a tricky, adversarial, or defensive dialogue ahead.

The way *you* view the impending conversation or your mindset towards it is another key element to the success of it. Are you worried about it? Do you imagine it will be confrontational? Do you doubt the outcome will be a positive one?

All of these negative thoughts mess with our psyche and our brain confirms.... this *will* indeed be challenging. This is going to be problematic. They will be demanding. The meeting will be tough. It's going to be uncomfortable.

These beliefs impact how we show up and behave. We might turn up metaphorically heavily armoured and ready for battle. Or conversely feeling like the underdog and wanting to shrink in the corner hoping it will be over before it began.

While we may not know for sure what others think, they will form their own impression of us. And if we are emitting negative or fearful vibes, that is exactly what will be picked up.

And then there is the question of approach.

If you haven't given much consideration to this, it would come as no surprise if you launched into the conversation mentally and physically unprepared. Bulldozing in like a bull in a china shop, unaware and oblivious to the impact this might stir, you may receive a taste of your own medicine and encounter a dose of belligerence back!

If you are irritated or frustrated, your impatience will ooze out into your conversation and the reaction might be a self-justifying and aggressive response taking you down another testing rabbit hole.

Or if you are a people pleaser and approach it too timidly, you may find others take advantage and walk all over you. Or they won't take you seriously, so the conversation never takes shape or picks up momentum and you leave it feeling frustrated, insecure, and deflated.

And this is what happened during a mediation I facilitated several years ago. The manager who called me in was an inexperienced lady who had been in post for about six months.

She was in charge of two employees who were polar opposites in culture, personality, values and work ethos. It was no wonder they didn't get on. However, they were part of the team, and it was imperative they found a way to work through their differences as it was impeding production of their project.

One of the employees was a tough *no-nonsense* type who had a great deal to say and certainly didn't hold back! She was a bully and had no fear to stand up to her new manager and if the truth be told, she showed little respect for her either.

So, when the manager tried time and again to intervene in their relationship breakdown with kindness, logic and all the endearing qualities of people pleasers, the conversation fell on deaf ears leaving the manager feeling quite inept and insecure, the bully more empowered and the other employee more upset.

I will talk more about people pleasing behaviours in Chapter 4 (The Three Archetypes) but for now, I think this illustrates that the way the conversation is approached can determine the tone for how it is received and how it plays out.

Exploratory and Journaling Questions:

1. Explore the reasons you find difficult conversations challenging.
2. Why do you think you avoid them?
3. Write a list of your biggest fears or limiting beliefs.
4. How do you approach difficult conversations?
5. List a few hot spots that might create friction in your approach.

2

AWARENESS

 "Awareness is a key ingredient in success. If you have it, teach it. If you lack it, seek it."

— *MICHAEL B KITSON*

I often think of conflict as a smouldering ember. Crackling and spitting purposefully under the surface, hidden below a hazy smoke. You can't quite see what's going on, but you can feel the intense heat rising from it. If you fan it, it will quickly plume. If you continuously stoke it, it will eventually catch and flare up. And this metaphor in my opinion beautifully emulates how a small prickly issue can spark a full-blown conflict. It's important to understand what you, or others do, that stoke these flammable situations to ignite the fuse.

And that starts with awareness of the factors that stimulate conflict so where possible, we can minimise the need for the difficult conversations in the first place.

I'm sure you've heard the expression; every action creates a reaction. Well this couldn't be truer in conflict.

I was recently invited to support a small family run business that was experiencing some friction between the business owner and a senior member of the leadership team. Being a small company, the impact of the relationship breakdown was impacting not just the other department heads and team members but also the family. Everyone had an opinion about the way it should be managed which only added to their stress.

The contentious issue was based on a conversation that almost every business globally has been discussing. The 'Return to Office' debate. Ahhh yes, that old chestnut! The problem however was not relating to other team members but expectations around the senior leader's hybrid working arrangements. Yet she and her boss were on very different pages on this moot point.

Because of the nature of her role, the senior leader was well informed and well versed in the minutiae detail of what she was permitted to do, she expressed this with great force to her boss.

Red flag. Round one.

The business owner was taken aback, shocked in fact at her brashness and attitude. So she adopted a defensive stance, doing what she thought was best at that time, which was to take legal advice to protect her position. She was *'reacting'* rather than acting from a place of considered thought which was to have a *'human conversation'* first in an attempt to constructively work it out between them and engage in an honest and respectful dialogue. Adult to adult.

When she hit back with her formal response and directive from the lawyers, it simply provoked another reaction.

Red flag. Round Two.

And so, it continued. Both were triggered, and both stayed firmly in their lane, entrenched in their beliefs and views. Neither side were willing to backdown or acknowledge each other's perspective which is very common in disputes. One side was protecting her value of reputation, while the other was seeking to have her values of justice and fairness acknowledged.

Values are a key driver in any dispute, and I will delve deeper into this in Chapter 7.

What's the lesson here?

This situation escalated at lightning speed because the business owner acted from a position of fear rather than engaging in a *'human conversation'* early on. A conversation that might have saved everyone stress, angst and worry and the organisation unnecessary financial and emotional costs as well as additional time that Board Members spent time trying to fix it.

Much like mediation is a recommended requirement in many business disputes before embarking on costly trials, I believe 'human conversations' should be a recommended requirement in every *business owner's handbook* when challenging issues crop up. They should be highlighted as a priority above any formal processes.

But it's not just individual human behaviours that contribute to conflict. There are extraordinary circumstances that contribute unwittingly to it too. Let's look at one of the most recent worldwide crisis. Covid-19.

As I have touched on in this previous example, the Covid-19 pandemic has played havoc with the working landscape and the following examples are just a few of many new problems that have come to the fore as a result of the crisis. Problems that leaders and business owners have been fervently addressing over the past few years.

Before the pandemic, it was more the exception rather than the norm to negotiate or even discuss flexible or agile working. Unless the role didn't necessitate it, employees generally worked Monday to Friday in the office, or place of work. It was a requirement and expectation that they turned up each morning. The team were all there, present, in one place at the same time, engaged and focused.

A phrase I've heard some leaders or business owners mention is the term *'It's a buyers' market'* when it comes to employee retention. What do I mean by that?

Pre-pandemic, their employees' hours and days were defined by the organisation. Unless there were extenuating circumstances or the role changed, that was that! It would have been quite unusual to enter into a negotiation around their 'in work' days.

Yet there has been a mighty shift. The pandemic has changed everyone's attitude to the working world. Today, if an employee is disgruntled about the days they are expected to come into their place of work, their attitude is to talk with their feet and join *The Great Resignation*. The bottom line (from their perspective), there's plenty of other organisations out there who will take them on their terms… hence… *It's a buyer's market*.

Wouldn't it be great if that changed and there could be more helpful dialogue around these situations?

The realisation that the wheels of industry could still continue to turn if their employees weren't office based, changed the working landscape. Leaders and management were faced with a new set of challenges and a plethora of potential conflict started to emerge and difficult conversations were popping up all over the place.

A huge number of business owners and leaders shared their

frustration and inability to effectively manage employees remotely.

Many conversations I have been party to were based on a deep-rooted lack of trust.

- Lack of trust that their teams were working the hours they were contracted to work.
- Lack of trust that their teams were working at all.
- Lack of trust they would meet targets or deadlines.
- Lack of trust they were engaged, focused or even at their desk rather than at the park with their children or taking their pet to the vet.

The only outcome from this mindset is a culture of suspicion and the behaviours the leaders demonstrated only serve to fuel a conflict.

So how does this show up? Micro-managing. This could manifest as a constant stream of check-up calls, an excess of draining virtual meetings and bombardment of emails all of which antagonise and trigger tension.

As we came out of the tail end of the first lockdown here in the UK in 2020, my husband and I were having dinner one night with an acquaintance. Naturally the conversation moved onto the pandemic, and we discussed how the last few months had affected his business.

He shared how brilliantly his team had approached the challenges of remote working and performance had increased significantly.

And then he continued to explain how he personally had daily check-ins to see how everyone was fairing. This really impressed me.

In addition, he rewarded each team member with morale-boosting token gestures such as a box of chocolates, a bottle of wine or gift vouchers which sounded very much like a caring, supportive and people centric culture.

And then... there it was.

Boom!

He disclosed that they had instilled new AI software to keep track of their teams and their productivity throughout the day. He announced with great glee how he sent one team member a 'notification' by way of a buzzer to alert her to the fact he knew she hadn't logged in yet at 9:00 am. And if she took too long for a toilet break... guess what... another buzzer!

I was horrified!

"Don't you trust your teams?" I asked.

"Yes of course!" He replied. But this keeps them on their toes. They have never been more productive!"

But at what cost?!

This just screamed out to me a culture of mistrust. You can dress it up with all the bells and whistles but at the end of the day, what's more important?

He never disclosed how many employees resigned as a result of this 'Big Brother' approach to management nor do I expect he would ever have shared the real data!

I will discuss in the following chapters the reasons leaders often tussle with micro-managing, what's behind this unhelpful management style and how to change that. However, a question to reflect on now is... are you *supervising* or *supporting* your teams? There is a big difference.

Another common issue I became aware of during the pandemic was those vital check-in meetings between leaders and their teams were far and few between. These were (and still are if your teams are working remotely) key to strong relationships. I'm not referring to weekly catch-up conversations about work but those *'human'* Monday morning chats at the water cooler, banter about your football team's performance over the weekend. Or those interactions in the kitchen waiting for the kettle to boil chatting about your children's exams, your baby's first steps or your elderly parent's health. Or even just asking how they are doing! The conversations that matter to your teams and connect you on a more personal level.

These are important dialogues that were so often forgotten or neglected during the pandemic. It's that old adage.... *Out of sight, out of mind*! Yet the message here or the conclusion your teams or colleagues might take from this is .... You don't care. You don't value them.

And from there, little pockets of resentment are harboured, bubbling away and sometime later and at a seemingly unrelated time in the future, it will pop up.... "You didn't ask me how my mother's operation went" or this example which I witnessed myself... "You knew I saw a specialist about my bad knee and yet you haven't even checked to see how it is. Just for your information, I have been told to take the load off it for now so I can't possibly stand for half an hour and photocopy all these documents!".

In this case the manager was both confused and irritated with her team member's attitude and couldn't understand why she was being so chippy about the photocopying. This all stemmed from the fact that her manager had failed to check in with her following her appointment with the doctor. In her opinion if her manager *'cared'* enough, she would have showed interest in her condition and would never have expected her to undertake this task.

You may think this is indulgent, but these small compassionate acts can make such a difference to relationships and change the course of a conversation and what consequently ensues in minutes.

When Things Go Formal

Unresolved issues can quickly escalate to formal processes which can trigger both tangible and intangible costs for managers or other senior leaders who spend countless hours investigating the problems. Time that could be spent far more usefully and productively on the business.

Another additional insight I have observed through years of mediating disputes within businesses is this. If a grievance is raised by a team member and the outcome of the investigation is not in favour of the complainant, that will increase the opportunity that they will not only still be *peeved* about the original grievance but now they will have 'beef' with the organisation for not 'taking their side'.

While this may be a distorted perception and the investigation outcome may have been a fair and just process, when your employees are tangled in the belief of *'being right and seeking justice'*, sometimes it is hard for them to comprehend that there could possibly be a different conclusion to the one they were expecting.

Now you have two problems to manage. A disgruntled employee with two proverbial axes to grind. The one against the organisation for not finding the grievance in their favour *and* a personal vendetta against you too for playing messenger, which doesn't bode well for future relations or karma within the business.

Another situation that rouses and escalates conflict is when grievances or disciplinary processes are poorly managed or investigations inappropriately performed. In some cases key people have been excluded from the investigative interviews and consequently not been allowed the *'the right to reply'*. Processes might not have been followed thoroughly or the approach may have been slapdash and poorly executed leaving those inextricably caught in the middle of it feeling unheard and that justice and fairness had definitely not prevailed.

There are a host of other organisational factors that play a part in conflict too which you might not have considered. If left unchecked or purposely avoided, they can provoke calamitous outcomes.

Change and Transition

Change, transition, growth, and expansion are exciting times within a business if you have been driving that evolution. Perhaps it's your own business or you're a leader who has been involved in those decisions and planning and therefore excited about the future.

However don't be surprised if your teams don't necessarily share in your enthusiasm. Change can bring up diverse emotions for everyone. While some people thrive on uncertainty, the excitement of the unknown and the freedom of unplanned adventures, for others (myself included) can stir anxiety. I am a planner, I like to know what's going on and how it's going to happen. For me, change feels very uncomfortable, and fear of the unknown is definitely a trigger.

When I first met my husband, I was in awe of his sense of adventure. His spontaneity. The fact that very little fazed him.

If his flight for an important business meeting was diverted or cancelled at the last minute, he would calmly find another one without panic or fuss, remaining level-headed and unflustered.

Me... not so much! That would have freaked me out and it's prompted many conversations where we often talk about our different approach to uncertainty in life.

Tell-tell signs that your team members aren't on board, willing or happy about the new way forward might show up as resistance, silence, pushback or overwhelm.

And the way that's managed will dictate the success of the changes. Simply telling them what a great plan it is and expecting them to jump on the bandwagon is probably not going to garner an influx of high fives!

New Management and People Dynamics

In order to grow the business, you will at some point bring in new managers or team members to support your evolution. However this is prime opportunity for potential conflict.

The way new people are introduced to the business can dictate the success or failure of their relationships and dynamics with the team. This might include expectations around the framework of their new role and what that looks like for the team. Let's look at this example.

You're a small business owner and you recruit a middle manager to alleviate some pressure from you on day-to-day operations while you focus on the bigger picture and business decisions. Yet the problem manifests as your teams are used to reporting into you and now they feel there is an obstacle blocking direct access to you. Resentment is in the room! You might experience a bit of attitude or find that your team members continue to seek you out and insist on side-stepping the new manager, creating a new wave of problems if you indulge this behaviour because the new manager feels undermined and resentful towards you.

And if your new recruit has been brought in to replace another manager, it wouldn't be uncommon for them to experience pushback and attitude from the team with comments like... 'This is how your predecessor did it!' So it's fair to say that if the introduction hasn't been carefully thought through and executed the new relationship will get off to a rocky footing with disrespectful and unhelpful behaviours showing up all over the place.

It's a political and sensitive minefield!

Or the new manager may adopt a different approach and management style which ruffles feathers. If you haven't invested enough time evaluating their personal values and whether they are aligned with your own values and those of the business, this can raise another red flag.

Misalignment of values is a big topic and the reason for an enormous amount of conflict I have seen over the years. And I will discuss more on this in part two of the book. However at this point, I will give you one more example you might not have considered around the hiring process.

If you are an entrepreneur just starting out and thinking about working with a freelancer or taking a virtual assistant on board, you might not have mapped out the specifics of your working relationship or garnered any clarity around the parameters, framework and expectations of this new association. While you may be a stickler for detail and deadlines, if your new recruit is more laid back and less interested in the finer minutiae, that's when the relationship might turn rocky.

However, this doesn't just relate to new managers. This is a process you might like to embrace with the recruitment of all your employees whether you are a large corporate or an entrepreneur hiring your first VA.

Implementing New Processes

I'm sure you will have heard the expression ...*'If it ain't broke, don't fix it!'*. This is often the resistant attitude that leaders face when they introduce new systems and processes to the business. While the reason behind them might have been explained with precision and clarity, some team members still might not acknowledge the need for it, happy to plod along doing things the same way they have been for years. Or they have little interest in learning it, particularly if it involves tech or complicated new-fangled procedures. And this is where you might have a fight on your hands.

Silos and Cross Functional Teamwork

When your teams work in silos it can generate an insular approach to their work and attitude. This might relate to entire departments across a large business, smaller teams working with external agencies or individuals keeping themselves to themselves. This singular approach means key information isn't shared creating havoc when one arm of the business is kept in the dark. It can impact projects that they are working on or entire schemes might need to be totally reworked or scrapped once the new information that comes to light... Just a bit too late! Months of planning and preparation down the can because people aren't communicating outside of their immediate environment. You can start to see the conflict picture emerge and understand how anger, resentment and frustration can so easily occur.

And then there is the problem of cross functional reporting when team members are managed by more than one boss across different departments. This can create confusion and spark resentment when each manager insists their work should take priority without consulting or communicating with the other managers leaving the employees helpless to try to make the best decision without upsetting their other bosses.

Boundaries

It's so important to create clear boundaries in working relationships but for some, this proves challenging. Many leaders or business owners I have worked with are natural born *people pleasers* and setting boundaries is a big ask for them for fear of upsetting their colleagues or teams and in some cases, clients.

But here's the problem; there are always consequences. Agreeing to longer deadlines on a piece of work that is already overdue might mean you miss your monthly targets. Allowing extra time off can incite resentment amongst the rest of team who have to pick up the slack. Committing to client projects when you are already stretched to the limit means another client project might suffer.

And what about boundaries when a colleague (who might also be a good friend) is promoted to become your boss. Navigating those new delicate dynamics and narratives can be very tricky if they are not managed skilfully and diplomatically.

Feedback

This is the topic I am probably asked about the most. How to deliver feedback and manage performance conversations without upsetting the apple cart. It is a mammoth subject and a topic I am dedicating a whole chapter to in part two.

Done well and it's plain sailing but delivered badly and it's one of the greatest causes and triggers of pushback, defensive responses, and confrontational behaviours.

Feedback is two-way of course and some leaders or business owners are reluctant to receive constructive critique of their own leadership style too. Perhaps because they are not open or willing to hear it, or simply not skilled in the habit of self-reflection. Or maybe the culture does not invite open and honest conversations or promote an ethos of psychological safety where all opinions are welcome.

Communication Style

We all have our own little nuances and specific ways that push buttons or irritate others. But our communication style is more than just the words that come out of our mouth, but our tone of voice and body language too. And it also relates to the way we respond to emails, the behaviour we exhibit when we are interrupted, the impatience we show when someone isn't listening or understanding our point. More about this is the next chapter!

If we are unaware of our idiosyncrasies and style and how they are received, we can spend our days in blissful ignorance of the impact of our unique ways on our teams and colleagues and in fact all relationships.

I hope it's becoming clearer that there are many contributing factors to conflict within businesses. Some human driven and some situational and circumstantial. However with a little awareness and intuition, we can avert them and prevent a small problem from spiralling into a crisis.

After all prevention is better than cure!

Exploratory and Journaling Questions:

1. List your top 5 core values.
2. What are your organisational values?
3. What is your biggest communication challenge with remote working?
4. What do you think contributes to conflict in your business?
5. How aware of these factors were you before reading this chapter?

3

COMMUNICATION

"The difference between mere management and leadership is communication."

— *WINSTON CHURCHILL*

Communication is such a vast topic on its own! Everything we say or do is a message. If we look at our phone during a conversation, it indicates we are disinterested. If we scroll through social media, whilst in the company of someone else, it informs the other person that *it's* more important than they are.

If we roll our eyes or look over someone's shoulder when they are talking, that's another message right there.

There is so much to consider. As I alluded to in the previous chapter, it doesn't just incorporate the words we use but our style and little nuances. Our tone of voice, our written and verbal interactions, our body language, our listening skills, our emotional state, our focus and presence and the way we show up. We need to be mindful too that different communication cultures can present a host of perils that disconnect and damage relationships.

This chapter is dedicated to exploring potential dangers that poor, unconsidered, impulsive, and inflammatory communication can present which elevates the threat of conflict.

Sometimes we are blissfully unaware of our style and spend our days '*doing communication*'!

What do I mean by that? Well, simply put, we don't consider how we communicate. We are robotic. We remain trapped in unhelpful habits. We are unaware of the ripple effect of a dialogue.

And let's be honest, unless there is a reason for us to explore our communication or we are particularly self-aware and *chose* to develop our skills, we wouldn't necessarily be conscious that our style is problematic.

However, whether you lead a team, run a business, or lead *yourself*, the way you interact with others will dictate the success or failure of projects. It will influence the quality of relationships with your colleagues, your teams and your clients. It will change the performance and productivity of those you work with and manage and impact the bottom line, the wealth of your business.... For better or worse!

So yes, it's very important to get it right.

Let's delve into communication pitfalls.

Communication Energy

At school I hated history! I was lousy at it and could never remember dates or battles or Kings or Queens. Until we were blessed with the most animated, engaging, funny and passionate history teacher. My love of history changed on that day.

I couldn't wait for the lessons and looked forward to them every week. I listened intently; I even did my homework!

Why?

Because our teacher was so engaging. She communicated at a level we all could understand and connect with. She brought the most amazing energy to the classes, and she *oozed* charisma and presence!

And her enthusiasm was contagious. We all performed brilliantly in our exams, and I have no doubt at all that this can only be attributed to her excellent communication and of course teaching skills which are intrinsically connected.

If I think back to other lessons, I was less enthusiastic about, most of the time, it was down to the dull and monotone delivery by the teachers.

I included this story because it illustrates the impact of good communication skills and how this wonderful history teacher effectively turned around a reluctant bunch of disinterested teenagers into high achievers! She motivated, she inspired, and she got the best out of us.

As a leader or business owner, isn't that what we all want?

As I indicated earlier, our communication is broken down into three parts which compose of verbal and non-verbal interactions; content and the words we speak (7%), our tone of voice (38%) and body language (55%).

The energy we bring to any conversation or the emotional 'state' we show up in, is so important and has more influence that we might imagine. When I refer to state, I'm not purporting to appearance, but presence. If you turn up to a meeting flat, deflated and sapping in energy, it wouldn't be unreasonable for your colleagues or teams to assume you were disinterested or bored. And from this observation they will draw several suppositions. You would rather be elsewhere. You aren't interested in what they have to say or the meeting.

If you're rushing between meetings, have been stuck in traffic, incensed by road works or diversions, you may arrive flustered, angry, and frustrated. This is the energy you bring into the room. As humans, we take this information, evaluate it, process it, and draw conclusions. In this scenario, the impression might be that you're flappable, out of control, disorganized, hot headed. If this was a client relationship you were trying to nurture or woe, your demeanour may just sway their decision in the wrong direction. The question they might ask themselves… "Would this be someone they want to work with?"

Emphasis and Expressions

Equally every inflection or enunciation of a word can denote a different meaning. It always makes me smile when I hear someone say, "I'm NOT angry", the emphasis being very heavily on the word '*not*' implying the exact opposite. Or my absolute favourite when you ask someone how they are, and they reply through gritted teeth …. "I'm FINE" and of course, they really aren't!

I will be focusing on these behaviours in chapter 8 but for now, the message here is to be aware of your intonation and mindful of your communication as the inference might not be what you meant at all!

As for facial expressions, the abundance of virtual meetings over the past few years has served to illustrate how little we focus on this area of communication. Like it or not, we have no choice (unless we and other attendees turn our videos off) to scrutinize every inflection and behaviour online.

However, some of us are oblivious that our faces often say more than words and portray our true thoughts.

This was very much the case during an online mediation last year that I was facilitating. It was at a poignant point towards the end of the day when I thought we were making good progress. I sensed they were inching towards a happier place.

Until one of the parties became stuck, labouring to find the right words to explain a point. She was struggling to open up and this vulnerability was uncomfortable and painful to observe. I could feel her pain and unease through the screen as I watched and listened.

Out of the corner of my eye I glanced towards the other participant, her manager, to gauge her reaction and saw in horror that her face was scrunched up in a scowl and her brow furrowed. The other participant, her report, noticed it too and flipped. All the headway we had made that day was destroyed in a matter of seconds. We had to take a break at that point because that one reaction caused such disruption, upset and turmoil that it would have been impossible to continue without addressing it.

We talked it through in a breakout meeting and what I found most interesting was the manager was totally unaware of the face she pulled at the time. However, the consequences of that one expression changed the course of the conversation and what ensued afterwards.

Sometimes we can lie with our words, but those micro-expressions give us away!

I heard another fascinating tell-tell sign about body language recently. Although this gem doesn't necessarily relate to conflict, I did love it and the message it carries is very useful so thought I would include it anyway! Next time you are in conversation at a networking event, have a quick look down at the other person's feet. Yes really! If they are pointing in your direction, this indicates they are engaged and interested in you. If on the other hand they are directed at the door (or anywhere but towards you), this signals they can't wait to make a swift exit! So, beware of this in your own interactions. If you see others staring down at your feet, you know what they are thinking!

Communication Style

So, let's take a look now at communication style. We all have our own unique way of communicating. This is the manner we share information, the language we use, frustrating nuances and habits we practice. It refers to the fashion we convey instructions. Whether our tone is too direct and blunt in email exchanges, or our approach is too subtle.

I heard a great story a few years ago about a business owner who asked his manager to address a problem with one of the team. The manager assured him he would get onto it and that he had a really good idea how to approach the conversation. A few days later the business owner bumped into the team member and asked how things were going. He said he thought all was well however he was a little confused about a conversation he'd had with his manager a couple of days earlier. He shared they'd had an interesting conversation about the rules of tennis but had no idea why!

The 'too subtle' approach illustrated beautifully!

Your communication might be a little *light* on details leaving the recipient confused and struggling to join the dots. Or you might fall into the category of 'chaotic' communicator, a *'last* minute Larry' blasting your teams with new tasks as they are about to leave for the day whipping up a cloud of frustration and anger.

Or maybe you are an 'over giver' bombarding your teams with too much detail in one hit creating overwhelm and panic. Or would you define yourself as an 'under giver' sharing the bare bones in a sequence of fragmented emails so they don't have adequate information to work with? Or perhaps your style is more akin to a stream of constant interruptions as you pop your head over the divider in the open plan office saying...."just one more thing!"

Another unhelpful communication style I encounter a great deal is something I refer to as 'Broadcasting Out'. What do I mean by that? You transmit out like a radio but don't receive back!

I'm sure we all know someone like that!

It's a style employed by some who talk *at* others rather than *with* them. They are so intent on putting their point across, they don't listen for (or hear) the reply back.

And let's be clear, communication is a two-way dialogue. I don't think it would be unreasonable to think a conversation like this might not end well!

As I mentioned earlier, our style is unique. If your message to your teams (or anyone) hasn't been understood or heard in the way you intended, this may be down to your particular style and as the Irish Comedian Frank Carson used to say.... *"It's the way I tell 'em"*.

We are all responsible for our own communication so if the message hasn't landed or the point missed, you will need to flex and adapt your style and approach so that it is understood loud and clear. A blame culture serves no-one.

Written Communication

The advent of so many new messaging platforms has led to a rise in impulsive and ill-considered communication. We all have a propensity to use this mode of communication much more but with hazardous consequences. Whatsapp, Voxer, Messenger as well as email of course all allow for instantaneous dialogue! How many of us have pressed send too quickly in an email or reacted recklessly in haste to a message?

However, this is where an abundance of misunderstandings and conflict can emerge. In these communications, no verbal or facial cues are present which only adds to spark reactive responses particularly when the point or tone of the message is often lost in translation in different formats.

The old-fashioned phone call seems almost archaic and outdated now. But my goodness it could save us all from time consuming and problematic messaging and email ping pong if it was used more frequently in these situations! Sometimes it would make life much less complicated to JUST *pick up the PHONE!*

Everyone has a predilection for how they prefer to receive information. While it may seem like an indulgence to bend to accommodate these preferences, it can be critical to a good or bad relationship. Some people respond well to verbal interactions while others would rather receive an email with information clearly outlined.

And this comes down to 'knowing your audience'. Do they curate brief, three-word emails themselves? In which case they would find a long-detailed reply back annoying to read if they bothered to read it at all.

Conversely, others might like long winded written explanations so would take a short email response as rude and blunt.

I have listened to bitter complaints about the way people begin and sign off emails which some would pay no attention to while to others it is of great significance. And this certainly raises the point around expectations of what is considered polite and normal behaviours in written communication.

Online Communication

It would be strange not to reference virtual communication since video meetings were our principle means of communication during the pandemic. I frequently heard grievances and gripes that it felt uncomfortable inviting people into the privacy of our home through our screens.

We are a nosy race and as we only have a few square inches to focus on, we search for things to pique our interest. We examined photos on the wall, we looked for clues about their lifestyle, the tidiness of their room, their choice of furniture or art. It is intrusive and invasive. Which is why people often chose not to turn their camera on and why zoom backgrounds became so popular. We judged and commented, and this created embarrassment and distress.

Communication Baggage

About fifteen years ago my twin boys were preparing for their *Bar mitzvah* and as part of their studies they were required to complete a number of voluntary community tasks called *Tzedakah*. And being twins, they undertook most of the assignments together.

To confirm completion of these undertakings, they met every couple of months with the Rabbi to show him what they had achieved and for their forms to be '*signed off*'.

One Friday afternoon, we arrived at the Rabbi's office and were shown in while he was still engaged on the phone. He didn't look up or even acknowledge our presence.

We sat there in silence for about ten minutes listening to his conversation that quite frankly we should never have been privy too. For both confidentiality and content. It sounded like a very difficult call.

He was upset and when the call ended, he abruptly said hello. He offered no apology for keeping us waiting, nor did he refer to the conversation.

The Rabbi was a large, intimidating grey haired American, towering over the boys with his burly six-foot frame.

He addressed the twins: "So, what have you got for me?"

With great gusto they both stood up and walked up to his desk. He scanned their work and then peered down at them over the rim of his glasses. I will never forget what followed.

He threw their sheets back at them and roared: "You've copied each other. Go back and do this again and find your own tasks next time!".

He then stood up, opened his office door, and dismissed us!

I was speechless! Furious. They silently left the office deflated, cross and upset.

As a leader of our community, I found his behaviour appalling.

The following Monday I made a formal complaint and requested the boys transferred to work with a different Rabbi.

To say I received a grovelling apologetic call from the Rabbi that day was nothing short of an understatement. He explained the conversation we had witnessed had been with a very dear friend who just been diagnosed with cancer.

While I understood his sadness and shock, in my opinion he should never have invited us in during the call but equally as important, he should have taken a few minutes to process the news and compose himself before our meeting began.

This is what I refer to as 'Communication Baggage'...The baggage and emotions you bring to a meeting without intention that can impact not just the direction of the conversation but more importantly, your relationships.

While this is quite an extreme example, it could be something as minor as the irritation caused by someone cutting you up in traffic or missing the train by a minute. You bring that 'baggage' with you into your communication and carry it around like a lead weight.

I'm delighted to say my boys were not scarred by this unpleasant event and are happy, thriving 27-year-olds!

Communication Behaviours

Communication is a behaviour. Dumping work on someone's desk. Arriving late to a meeting. Beckoning with your finger to invite someone to join a conversation. Refusing to turn on your camera in a video meeting. Holding your hand up to show you don't want to be interrupted right now. Shutting your office door while you're on the phone when someone is about to walk in. These are all communication behaviours that we might just think of as... *well this is just who I am*. But have you stopped to think how they are being experienced by others and what this denotes to them?

Equally the behaviours of others are a communication too.

And there's so much more to explore and discover on this subject later in the book.

The Message of No Communication

One of my most challenging mediations I facilitated a few years ago was a complex situation where concerns were raised by colleagues about the behaviour of one of the directors. For the purpose of this story I will change his name to John.

The manager (who I will refer to as Emily) was coordinating the investigation into the alleged issues although no formal grievance was raised. The conclusion was that there was no evidence to suggest any misconduct however it left a bitter taste and bad feeling between John and his team. John resented the complaint and the backhanded way it had been raised and his team were still uncomfortable with his management style and behaviours.

I was brought in once these inquiries had been undertaken to help repair the damage and build relationships again.

However, there was one big problem that seemed too tough a mountain to overcome. During the process, Emily had promised to come back post investigation to John following her conversation with the Faculty Director, Amanda, and keep him informed about next steps.

Yet she didn't. And John was left in the dark for weeks, wondering, worrying, waiting. It started to affect his own mental health, percolating his thoughts with all possible outcomes, impacting his sleep patterns, his behaviours with colleagues, his relationships outside of work and eventually his professional judgement. He was confused and angry.

When this came up during one of the mediation meetings,

Emily casually brushed over it dismissing the magnitude and impact this period of uncertainty had placed on him.

"Well, it was only three or four weeks", she quipped back.

It was not a moment I care to experience again. Her nonchalant reply provoked a volatile reaction and I understand why. While the conversation was marked on her 'to do' list, it moved further down as other issues took priority. She then took a week's holiday leave, planning to discuss it with John on her return. By which time he was so tormented with worry and fear that he was straining to function effectively in his role.

When I asked Emily why she didn't do as she promised and keep John informed, she shrugged it off dismissively, nonchalantly, repeating again that it had only been a few weeks. And this is where perspective is a useful tool. More about this later.

Let's just say the culture at this organisation might have benefited from a review and a bit of a shake up!

So, take heed. The message of no message can stir up a storm!

Communicating During a Crisis

Knowing the best way to approach difficult communications was on everyone's 'how to' list during the global pandemic. And it certainly wasn't easy.

Challenging and sensitive conversations were required around the health and longevity of the business, redundancies, the impact on jobs, emotional health, and personal circumstances as well as of course empathetic chats with those who contracted Covid-19 themselves.

This was unchartered territory. There was no handbook to reference. Leaders were vacillating about their options moving forward. Many had little-to-no experience knowing what to say or do during this time. Some bore a 'Teflon Tough' mask and approach while secretly harbouring fear for the future.

Others muddled their way through sporadically checking in with their teams who were either furloughed or key workers still in their place of work. Either way, their communication lacked presence, clarity and gravitas leaving many of their employees to draw misguided assumptions about the business and security of their role, nurturing mistrust, and panic.

And then of course there was a plethora of compassionate conversations addressing emotional health issues with teams and colleagues which many leaders were inexperienced, uncomfortable, or ill-equipped to manage so either avoided or handled badly. They tip-toed around these situations worried, uncertain, and fearful that they might rock the applecart if their communication was 'too much' or 'not enough'!

As for the leaders and business owners' own individual emotions and state, they were wracked with fear and alarm. Life was a rollercoaster ride. Some days they were hopeful and the next day they felt hopeless. And this is what they inadvertently projected if they didn't check in with themselves and how they were showing up!

And then there were the conversations where they tried to paper over the cracks. To pretend that everything was fine. But what their words expressed their behaviours defied. The inauthentic persona roused mistrust leaving teams wondering what was really going on!

Communication and Different Cultures

Cross-cultural communication is a potential conflict hotspot.

In many western cultures eye contact is seen as a sign of sincerity, warmth, and respect, yet in others, it is considered the opposite. And this same principle is true with gestures of greeting like a handshake. For Jewish orthodox women is it is forbidden for them to engage in this custom with men, while a firm grip in other cultures signifies strength and confidence.

Bear in mind too that in some Asian cultures, it is considered disrespectful and inappropriate to disagree or challenge a superior. This presents a problem if you are hosting an open table discussion inviting opinions from your teams yet they remain silent, fearful to speak honestly or to appear challenging. It's hard to coax a change when this is an inbred cultural behaviour but there are ways round this which I will address in Chapter 10.

This also presents opportunity for costly misunderstandings in written communication where the meaning and intention is lost in translation.

Be cautious too of how you apply humour in written formats, particularly if the recipient is a new acquaintance. Without informative visual cues such as a smile, they may miss the comic element in your communication. This is something that I have been guilty of myself which caused some embarrassment!

Communication presents a minefield of potential conflict opportunities but if you are tuned into them, you can avoid and navigate them with success!

Exploratory and Journaling Questions:

1. How would you define your communication style?
2. If you asked your team or colleagues one thing they would change about your communication, what do you think it would be?
3. What communication baggage have you been guilty of carrying?
4. What did you find challenging about communicating with your teams and colleagues during Covid-19 or any other crisis?
5. Has cross cultural communication presented a problem in your business and in what way?

4

THE THREE ARCHETYPES

> "I can't tell you the key to success, but the key to failure is trying to please everyone."
>
> — ED SHEERAN

Throughout my years of coaching, training, consulting, and mediating, I noticed that it's not just the *way* we show up for difficult conversations that can energise a conflict but *who* we show up *as*.

We are complex. That's for sure.

I believe there are elements of three *Archetypes* that influence leadership communication. This may sound like a huge generalization but it's simply my observation.

This doesn't mean they morph into their labels but that elements of their communication are shaped by these Archetypal characteristics.

So, who are they?

The People Pleasers. The Warriors. The Freshers.

Perhaps you recognise yourself in one of them?

Leadership is not a 'one size fits all' style or approach. However in my experience, there are fragments from every one of these Archetypes that infiltrate our dialogues and relationships. And unless we are conscious of their part in our communication, it might present one of the biggest obstacles to fruitful conversations and thriving relationships.

So, let's examine these three Archetypes and analyse how each leadership style shapes our communication and the way we lead, contributes to discord, and impacts dynamics.

The People Pleasers

If you are a *People Pleaser*, engaging in a confrontational conversation or approaching a situation that you believe might trigger a challenging or prickly reaction can be terrifying.

And I know because I am one.

I'm an *over giver* yet this virtue has also been a hindrance for me too. I concede too easily when I should have been more assertive. I offer too much of myself and my time without charge. I struggle to set clear boundaries. I am too available. I have often kicked myself for agreeing to take on projects or joining costly memberships because I don't want to offend. And I have fluffed up feedback if I think honesty will be met with hostility.

And all this has achieved is internal conflict, resentment, frustration for me and friction in my professional relationships. Yet through the work I do, I have observed the damage it generates, and I realized that if I plan to support others overcome these communication hurdles, I will have to walk my talk. I am a work in progress!

A difficult conversation for a *People Pleaser* can rouse anxiety, panic, fear, and all sorts of unhelpful mind chatter about what might happen if...

The issue however is that as a leader or business owner, those straight-talking dialogues are essential. We can't afford to pass them over. Or if we do and they don't go to plan, there are consequences.

In leadership this thoughtful, kind-spirited and generous trait is both an attribute and an impediment. One of the greatest fears for this Archetype is upsetting others. As I have alluded to above, *People Pleasers* grapple with the word 'no' or struggle to dish out direct feedback which leaves others not only confused but also mistrusting and resentful. However as a leader or business owner, your role demands honesty Your team deserves it.

A mediation several years ago demonstrated the fall-out from absent and honest feedback to the detriment of all relationships. The MD, Penelope, supervised two team members. Neither liked each other. Helen had a sharp tongue and terse manner. Sally was her recently appointed manager who was new to the organisation and attempting to make a good impression on her superiors. She was operating with a little too much gusto and not enough grace. And it was like *Clash of the Titans*!

As you might imagine, small irritations between them evolved into more volatile exchanges, until it became untenable to the point that they could no longer work together in a professional manner.

Penelope was instated as Helen's manager to act as a buffer between them in their interactions. Penelope, being a *People Pleaser*, found it awkward to directly express her concerns about Helen's aggressive communication style at the risk of upsetting her and the fear of hostile pushback she might be subjected to. So never brought it up.

However, during the mediation, Helen's truculent style began to creep into the conversation.

Sally piped up with: "You see, this is exactly what I mean and the reason why Penelope finds it hard to manage you too!"

Ouch! That set the cat amongst the pigeons.

Accusations of lies were hurled about along with stammering of utter disbelief. We took a break and during those fifteen minutes it transpired that Helen had phoned Penelope to question this contentious allegation. Her manager *conveniently* missed the call, but we subsequently heard she certainly suffered a smattering of *egg on her face* when the truth was finally revealed. Penelope was offered coaching to support her management style but declined.

This was a sad but common example of a *People Pleaser* who was afraid to share candid feedback offering those she managed what she thought would be easier for them to hear (and her to deliver) not what they needed to hear. And I think it's evident how this furthered the relationship breakdown for all concerned.

I have also experienced situations where a leader or business owner has been afraid to speak up and intervene in team conflict, cautiously sitting on the fence, hiding, secretly worried that their teams won't like or respect them if they appear to take sides. So in their opinion, it would be *safer* to take a step back and do or say nothing in the hope it will settle down. It rarely does.

Or they opt for what I refer to as the *'pandering'* approach. What do I mean by that? When two team members individually approach you complaining about the other and you pander to each of them with the *inference* that you agree, offering suggestions of 'You know what x is like' without doing anything constructive to manage the problem. However, in your opinion you have listened *and* saved your bacon by retreating from the conversation unscathed and free from scrutiny and pushback... which for a *People Pleaser* is a win. For the situation with your teams... not so much!

It's a game of chance. You play one off against the other until one day they do speak to each other, and the proverbial s**t *hits the fan*. Your teams don't know who or what to believe creating a culture of mistrust.

Another pattern of *People Pleasing* behaviour is an inability to say 'no' which I mentioned above. It can send shockwaves and leads to challenging responses and resentment if your teams are accustomed to always hearing the sweet sound of yes. It also generates confusion and disbelief leaving them wondering what's changed in your relationship that you have morphed overnight into such a tyrant! Well, the simple truth is that nothing will have changed except the implementation of some boundaries and new skills to manage the situation more competently and comfortably.

If you're a small business owner or entrepreneur, the absence of 'no' in some of your client conversations can also take its toll on relationships too if your boundaries are pushed to take on additional work outside of the remit of your contract. You might agree to it without additional payment but with consequences. Your client might continue to take advantage of your goodwill while you feel resentful, less gracious, committed, or enthusiastic to complete it. It's fair to say that piece of work probably won't be your best and you will ultimately let yourself and your client down.

Or perhaps you blunder clumsily through those potentially confrontational conversations chasing late or non-payment of your fees leaving you upset, the client irritated and your invoice unpaid.

If you are a *People Pleasing* entrepreneur, managing performance conversations with your VA or small team can also present challenges and impact output as well as growth of your business.

You might skirt around the issue but never get to the core of it. An example of this came to light last year when a client consulted me about the most helpful way to approach a situation with her new assistant around her 'to do' list that never appeared to reach a finite end. She was hesitant to discuss it, concerned that she would manage it indelicately provoking a hostile interaction and the dawn of a great big chasm in their professional relationship.

What she did do however was ask her assistant how she was getting on with it... and then simply left it at that without exploring the situation in any more detail. She was afraid to challenge her on the incomplete tasks or points that hadn't even been activated. So her frustration increased, resentment bubbled away, eating her up and achieving no constructive conclusion.

And what about when your boss or colleagues seek your expert opinions, and you simply agree with them for fear of offending with an adversarial view. Yet these tactics serve no-one. You feel unfulfilled because you have so much you would love to contribute, and your boss never appreciates your value so your chances of the next step up the corporate ladder will be thwarted.

Finally, there is the unnerving conversation of tackling bullying behaviour. This isn't an easy one for anybody but for *People Pleasers*, the fear it generates can be magnified tenfold. If it's not managed quickly and competently there is a risk that the toxic behaviours continue and are accepted as the norm, while those impacted by the harassment remain distressed and tormented.

So, as you can see, there are penalties associated with this Archetype which contribute to conflict and in some extreme cases, might lead to the escalation of a personal vendetta against you. Don't be disheartened however! Remember this part of the book is dedicated to the awareness of conflict and prevention. You will find support, solace, and antidotes to these problems in Part 2…Cure!

The Freshers

I remember as a child the feeling of trepidation at school, tentatively putting my hand up to ask a question. Looking around the classroom for a clue or an encouraging nod from a classmate that I was on the right track.

I'd feel my cheeks flush with embarrassment if the question brought a flurry of laughter from my classmates or a stern response from my teacher.

The fear of ridicule or judgement outweighed my thirst for knowledge. So I gradually stopped asking.

If you're a newly promoted manager or even an entrepreneur hiring a team for the first time, the same may be true. You might feel unsure of yourself or inept at addressing challenging behaviours because you believe there is an expectation that you should have the skill set to manage them.

You fear mockery or judgement if you mismanage these tricky conversations. That it will cloud opinions of your leadership ability. So, you keep quiet or dance around the issues. And as you climb the leadership ladder it becomes more embarrassing to ask for training or support, so you continue in this vein until a crisis blows up and you have no idea what to do!

This is not an isolated example of new leadership.

But let me just ask you a question here. In which book does it tell you that you should be expected to have all the answers as a novice manager or have the skillset to manage people? None that I have read. So, relax and breathe... (cue smile here).

However, my purpose here is to highlight the potential red flags that *Freshers* should be conscious of and to encourage them to use this as a learning platform to prevent these situations evolving either through awareness, training or asking for support from someone more experienced.

The transition from your previous role into this new role is not without complication. People management is a whole new function on its own and the mistakes I have witnessed in many organisations is an expectation that if you excelled in your previous job, you will be an expert at managing people too. This can be applied of course to any new business owner or entrepreneur who has never led a team before. You might have a brilliant business and assume your people management skills match your business prowess.

Big mistake... Huge! (This is a reference to one of my favourite films *Pretty Woman* and if you have seen it, you will understand this perfect moment... but I digress!)

This is often where the new relationship starts to fall apart before it's begun. There is an innate fear that you don't really know what you're doing. And that may be true. You might be a little nervous, anxious. And I as I mentioned in the Chapter 3 on communication, it impacts how you show up and lead your new team.

Confidence in leadership is key. However if you don't

believe in your own skills or ability, it's unlikely others will too. And here is where it can impact your communication in meetings and 1:1's with not just your teams but your peers, clients and your own manager. Because to be taken seriously you need to garner respect, command authority and exude gravitas.

Let me explain.

If you manage a razor sharp team, there's a high risk they will sniff out your fear and use this to their advantage. Requests for unscheduled time off (that isn't really permitted) will creep into your inbox. You might notice several team members skive off early or clock in late here and there which will become the norm not the exception. An extended lunch break will become more frequent because they know they can get away with it... and you might be a little uncomfortable to reprimand this behaviour (after all you want them to like you!) However, respect will be lost if it was even present in the first place. Until the situation reaches crisis point.

And then on the opposite end of the spectrum, you might show up as *Teflon Tough*. This is the mask you carry to hide your insecurities and lack of confidence however it just does not sit well with your teams or bring out the best in them. That tough exterior will bristle and ruffle feathers and does nothing to build rapport and trust. In fact it will create mistrust and barriers between you.

While you may be delighted at your new promotion, there are others who may not be as excited or enthusiastic as you. I'm referring to a former friend or colleague who now reports *into you* and who might also have been in the running for the job you now fill. And that can be a thorny relationship to steer through.

This transition to their new boss is a tricky one to navigate and can create some awkward conversations if it isn't managed sensitively and with a good measure of EQ. There are a number of problems that can arise from the new relationship that necessitate some skilful handling, or you will more than likely experience a rift in your friendship or difficulties in your role as their new manager if you don't engage in an honest conversation about the new dynamics and set clear boundaries.

Like the *People Pleasers*, managing team conflict or defiant behaviours is not without challenge. Even if you have progressed further up the leadership ladder, this can be a formidable undertaking. Knowing what *to* say and what *not* to say can be a minefield. Sidestep it and it hangs around seeking out others to fuel the drama. Mismanage it and it quickly spirals out of control.

The outcome of both these actions (yes avoidance is a choice action!) means *Freshers* never really delve deep into issues and only respond to surface level problems but not what is at the core. They brush over challenging conversations leaving those caught up in the crossfire feeling unheard and stuck wondering where to go with all this unaddressed anger and upset. Sometimes this will be the straw that broke the camel's back and they will feel they have no choice but to raise a formal grievance, taking up more of your time in the investigation and inevitably stirring resentment from your teams that you didn't step in and step up either.

Inexperience can also be a barrier to drive and motivate teams, leaving your teams uninspired, plodding along without any KPI's, goals, targets, and incentives. Navigating performance conversations (particularly with former colleagues) can present obvious difficulties and pushback in your feedback process if respect is lacking and your observations are ignored. All of which results in the conversation ending on a sour note with no helpful conclusion reached, no progress made, or no course of action agreed.

Freshers are often faced with a situation they feel inept to manage, particularly if their teams look to them for direction that they can't provide. Sometimes they think they are doing the right thing by attempting to bluff their way through, making all the right noises and promises to take action but they simply do not follow through on their commitment. And that's where mistrust will crop up time and again. It only takes one strike in the early days for impressions to be made which will define their leadership skills and relationship moving forward.

And finally, what about those uncomfortable compassionate conversations with your teams who are struggling with their emotional and mental health, poor physical health or tough personal circumstances which can go awry with devastating consequences if skill, empathy and listening skills are not yet developed. These will never be easy interactions for all concerned but probably more uncomfortable if your team member is talking to their new manager or boss who has absolutely no idea what to say!

I hope I've evidenced how inexperience can influence and energise conflict and uncomfortable conversations for *Freshers*. However Part 2 will offer guidance and support to navigate these potential hotspots with confidence.

The Warriors

When I worked in PR many moons ago, I remember one particular boss who I loved working for. He was firm but fair. Compassionate, considerate, empathetic, kind, supportive, respectful, and nurturing.

He was a brilliant leader and brought the best out in all of us. The department was a well-oiled wheel with him at the helm, smoothly run and thriving.

It was little wonder that he was soon promoted, and his replacement stepped into a very big pair of boots that she didn't come close to fill.

She was tyrannical, *Teflon Tough,* and not particularly kind. She had high expectations of all of us, yet we often seemed to disappoint her.

Why was this?

We certainly hadn't changed but the circumstances had. When she demanded that we do things differently to her predecessor, she was often met with resistance or pushback.

"This is how do it now!" was a response we heard from her all too often.

She thought we were all difficult, yet she didn't quite grasp that her bullish and detached style didn't ingratiate, motivate, or nurture. And she failed to appreciate that if she had invested some time in developing some rapport and connection with us, the road ahead might have been less bumpy. We would have been on board, aligned and more willing to embrace her initiatives.

And this is where *Warriors* miss a trick. Because the power of strong relationships, connectivity and empathy can certainly bolster professional pathways, drive performance and enhance productivity.

As *Warriors* are business focused and not people focused, they fail to spot the early warning signs if their teams are stressed or in need of help. They may conveniently *pass* on these 'heart to hearts' as they believe it's not their role to interfere ... until it impacts their work. Either way, their reports feel unsupported, and those delicate conversations can often end in carnage leaving them to conclude that their *Warrior* boss is cold-hearted.

A critical conversation often overlooked but vitally important is praise and recognition for a job well done or appreciation for extraordinary effort. Yet this doesn't come naturally to the *Warrior* which leaves teams feeling deflated, demotivated, unvalued and unproductive. And if this continues, it will come as no surprise if your teams look elsewhere for a business where they do feel valued and acknowledged.

Warriors are passionate leaders and business owners on a mission to drive the business or department forward. Yet that *over*drive can get them into some hot water. I've often seen this with middle management brought in when the business is going through a bit of a shake up or change. It's an unsettling and disruptive time for those working in it so the *Warrior* presence and combative approach feels even more unnerving.

And if this is your own business, you might be running at 100 mph expecting others to keep up with your ideas and pace. Pushing, waiting, and wondering why they can't match your energy and speed because *they assured you*, they were fast workers during their recruitment interview. But everything is relative. In their previous role, fast paced to their former boss might have been snail's pace to you. There's a wonderful quotation by the comedian George Carlin:

"Have you ever noticed that anybody driving slower than you is an idiot, and anyone going faster than you is a maniac?"

The relevance here is… what's your normal? Because we all have a different point of reference. And if you are running on a different trajectory and journey to your teams, there is likely to be an impatience and intolerance if they don't keep up. This is irritating for you, pressurising for them and problematic for your relationship.

Like my former boss, and in complete contrast to *People Pleasers*, some *Warriors* can be quite plain-spoken and deliver feedback a little too harshly without considering the impact of their ways. The intention is never to offend but to be crystal clear. However, it can trigger defensive responses or the opposite, suppressing honesty, prompting others to shut down, recoil and afraid to speak up.

This Archetype can be problematic in disagreements with colleagues and business partners too, particularly if the sole purpose is to dogmatically prove a point and there is a reluctance to listen to others. Business decision and planning can become dysfunctional and brought to a frustrating halt if *Warriors* spend more time clashing, poking the bear and arguing than they do strategizing.

And then there are the *Warriors* who arrive late to meetings and take over as if it's theirs to chair. They launch into conversations like a bull in a china shop, stepping on toes with their bristling style. At other times, they interfere in conversations or a chain of email communication that doesn't necessitate their contribution. Blowing up smoke and stirring up trouble.

This *Warrior*, although hugely motivated, driven and bringing great value to the health of the business, can in contrast be very problematic to the health of your relationships with your teams, colleagues, and clients.

So, the question is, do you recognise a *teeny tiny* element of any of these Archetypes in your communication? If so, it might be an opportune time for some self-reflection to consider who you show up as and how your style contributes to those thorny conversations that rock the status quo.

Exploratory and Journaling Questions:

1. Do you recognise any elements of your leadership in these three Archetypes?
2. Do you think your colleagues, business partners or teams would agree?
3. How does it impact your relationships and the business?
4. On reflection, what do you think you could change?
5. What steps are you going to take now to effect those changes

5
ASSUMPTIONS AND EXPECTATIONS

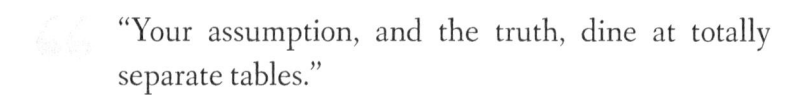

"Your assumption, and the truth, dine at totally separate tables."

— J MICHAEL STRACZYNSKI

Assumptions. Assumptions! That old chestnut. And we all know what they are the mother of!

It's amazing how misguided theories can ruin perfectly solid relationships in a matter of minutes. Our brain works in an interesting way. If we don't have the facts at our fingertips, we build our own narrative about what we see and hear. Like a jigsaw puzzle we like to piece fragments together to make a story. But in business relationships this is dangerous and destructive and I will illustrate why throughout this chapter.

Sitting alongside assumptions are expectations which I consider are intrinsically connected and can muster up as much damage as their counterpart, assumptions.

Let's then explore how these behaviours can infiltrate our thought process, impact management of performance conversations and trigger tiny pockets of doubt or misunderstandings leading to, you guessed it... conflict and discord.

Assumptions and Feedback

Last year I facilitated a dialogue between a manager and her assistant. The contentious point was the way the manager shared feedback with her about a document she had prepared for a client. On completion she emailed it to her boss to sign it off however it was sprinkled with errors and instead of just pointing them out, she suggested her assistant scan through it once more with a fine toothcomb.

Which she did.

But she still couldn't locate her mistakes. So she asked her manager again to share what they were.

And she was met with the same answer which wasn't really very helpful.

The manager's thought process was this. She *assumed* her assistant would easily spot the errors (which she believed were glaringly obvious) and that once she had, she would take note and remember them the next time because she had invested time and energy to seek them out herself on this occasion.

Well, as you might have imagined, it didn't pan out like that!

The assistant's answer was: "I've really tried, but I'm not a mind reader!".

What followed was a confusing, frustrating and time-consuming exchange of emails over a period of two days all of which could have been explained and addressed in minutes over a quick phone call. Which is eventually exactly what *did* take place!

The manager's assumption was way off track, as was her management of the situation.

Next time you assume your team members can mind read, remember this tale and think again!

Assumptions and Onboarding

An issue I am often asked to consult about is managing problems onboarding new team members or even working with VA's if you are a small business. Now we are all very busy, prioritizing projects and workload, juggling balls in the air, serving our clients and building profitable businesses and so our focus might not be on easing our new hire into the role. And perhaps there's an unrealistic expectation that they will seamlessly transition into the new role without much direction or input from you. Wishful thinking!

But here's where it becomes tricky. You will of course know how your systems operate and how you prefer your presentations to look or your Trello boards to be set up.

But have you scheduled time out to explain all this to your new hire? Because if they get it wrong or it hasn't been executed how you like it, that's down to your misguided assumption that they *should* know what to do. And an inability from you to put yourself in their shoes, sit on the other side of the table, get inside their head, and view it from their perspective.

Be wary of assuming that just because they might have performed these tasks in their previous role that your systems and methods for completing them are the same. Because they won't always be.

Assumptions and Abilities

Even if your team member has been in post for a long period, expectations around abilities can still present complications.

There are some things we excel in and others we find more challenging. And that's not necessarily a problem unless there is an expectation that your team member *should* know how to skilfully complete assignments *because* of their experience.

A few years ago, this point came to the fore during a mediation with a new Department Head and a senior member of her leadership team who had been with the organisation for around ten years. As he was a long serving employee who had climbed the corporate ladder, his new boss's assumption was understandably that he was proficient in proposal writing.

So, when she continued to challenge his competency and slate his work, it generated some heated exchanges between them.

His boss simply couldn't fathom or accept why, after his extensive stretch in that role, his work was so shoddy and lacked substance in content, presentation and detail. After some awkward and humiliating revelations, it transpired he avoided proposal writing at every opportunity, not only because he disliked it and found it taxing but also because he had never received any support or training to master it in all the years he had worked there.

What also came to light from this conversation, compounded the issue and added to his boss's frustration and impatience was she found proposal writing *effortless* so assumed everyone else *should* to! A faux pas that nearly broke that relationship.

Assumptions and Ambiguity

Another reason you might encounter tension in your communication is ambiguity. How often have you sat through 1:1's or team meetings and asked everyone if they have understood at the close of the conversation? They all smile and nod enthusiastically leaving you with the impression (and assumption) that everyone knows what they are doing. Happy Days!

Until that next chance meeting in the corridor or check in call when you ask how that task is coming along and they look at you blankly, shifting uncomfortably from one foot to the other.

If you don't clarify timelines, pin down specifics and confirm details they will be left with a vague notion of when the piece of work needs to be completed by and exactly what that might looks like. This is their assumption which may be poles apart from yours.

So, whose responsibility is it to confirm these minutiae details? Yours!

Assumptions and Accountability

I wish I had a penny for the number of times I have witnessed many heated exchanges over the years that all begin with..." But I thought you were doing it!"

Now *it* could relate to a few things. It might be responsibility for writing up meeting notes, calling a client, making amendments to a document, seeking a quote from a supplier.

Sound familiar?

And the question is why did you think that? Was it agreed by all those party to the discussion? Or was that your unfounded assumption?

And this is how it might have played out. You are absorbed in a meeting with colleagues or business partners, working your way through the agenda, when your attention is drawn to a new point raised by a colleague. Distracted, the discussion moves on in a new direction however responsibility for actioning the previous point remains undecided while you all *assume* someone would take care of it.

The meeting continues and responsibility for that point is still left hanging.

And it might not be until sometime later that it rears its' ugly head when one of you enquire.... What did the client say? Or is that document now complete? Or how much did that quote come in for? Do you see where this is going?

And then the accusations fly.

"You mentioned checking in with the client in the meeting so I *assumed* you would take care of it". Or... "You said we should get three quotes, so I *presumed* you had people in mind to ask!"

And so, it continues, the finger of blame pointed in all directions and inflammatory accusations hurled because no-one took responsibility for the task at the time of discussion.

Making Assumptions about Behaviours

If you recall in Chapter 3, we deconstructed Communication Baggage. And here is a perfect example of how the '*communication weight*' we carry around with us can inspire an untrue narrative about what's going on. I have used a hypothetical example based on a real situation, but I think it illustrates beautifully the domino effect of *assumptions* in action!

David was catching up with his colleague Michael one

Friday lunchtime in the cafeteria over a coffee. The company they worked for had been navigating some turbulent times during the previous six months.

He happened to mention he'd seen their CEO *storm* out of the Finance Meeting earlier in the day looking brow beaten and drained. They casually discussed it for only a few minutes moving quickly on to the customary banter about their football teams.

This innocuous observation was overheard by another colleague in the queue and repeated to *her* lunch partner, who some time later shared it with another team-mate.

Within a few hours… boom… the entire department was discussing '*it*' and the issue had snowballed. Was the business in jeopardy? Were redundancies on the horizon? Several people spent the weekend deeply concerned about the security of their jobs, frantically updating their CV's, scouring LinkedIn for job opportunities and by Monday lunchtime some had even arranged a few interviews!

And all this originated from the reference to the CEO's demeanour as he hurriedly left his meeting with the 'Money Men'! Quite an assumption.

But let's just rewind this back.

Who knew for certain why the CEO left the meeting in that manner? Perhaps a personal issue had drawn him away. The point is that somewhere along the line of communication, it had been *assumed* that redundancies were on the cards because the CEO left his meeting with finance looking deflated and upset. That was their narrative.

No-one knows for sure. But what we do know for sure is that assumptions were made based on his behaviour and without substantiating the facts. And that created unnecessary panic.

Assumptions During a Crisis

Throughout lockdown here in the UK, I heard many sad tales of businesses going through desperate times. Communication during that period was crucial to keep employees in the loop about developments, both good or bad.

While some business owners and leaders quickly grasped the importance of this, many did not. Their focus was striving to keep the business afloat not on communication with their people. However, this presented a chasm in relationships because those critical check in conversations were few and far between leaving teams and departments in the dark. And as is the way during communication blackouts, people draw their own conclusions from the absence of information and create their own fiction about what was really going on.

Just before the pandemic, I went to see a fantastic show in London at the theatre called 'Come from Away'. It's based on the true story of the 9/11 terrorist attacks that shook the world when 38 planes were diverted to a small airport in Newfoundland Canada, following the closure of US Airspace.

The planes, carrying just over 6,000 passengers or 'The Plane People' (as they were duly named), landed at Gander Airport, where they were grounded for nearly thirty hours with a complete news blackout. In order to avoid rising panic and fear, the passengers were told absolutely nothing about what had happened or why they were there.

What must they have been thinking? What did they imagine had happened? Because that's all they could do. Imagine and assume the absolute worst without being in possession of all the facts.

And this was a story I often shared with my clients during

the pandemic. *They* had a choice and were in control of what they could communicate. Those pilots of the thirty-eight planes did not. And that must have been terrifying.

So, this led me to think about what happens in times of crisis and uncertainty when your teams are kept in the dark? Because as I explained at the start of this chapter, when we don't know answers we fabricate our own storyline, based on past experiences or limited knowledge. We become suspicious. And that's when rot starts to set in which can corrode confidence and trust.

Assumptions, Friendships and Family

Friendships and family relationships in the workplace can be tricky. Old friends, new friends, brothers, fathers, sons, daughters, mothers, sisters. It can become caustic when there's an assumption or expectation that you will support your friend or family member, even if you don't agree with their conduct or opinion. You might find yourself sitting between a rock and a hard place. Loyalty feels challenged and it becomes personal and complex to navigate.

I can only equate it to an 'unsaid code' that you will back each other come what may. However I have seen the fall out when this code has been broken and it's much harder and more delicate to navigate than a disagreement with a colleague.

Perhaps you've been there yourself?

I experienced this uncomfortable situation a few years ago facilitating a conversation between who two friends who had known each other for years. They enjoyed BBQs and pub lunches with their respective partners. Their children, who were very young played at each other's houses together and attended each other's birthday parties. It was a lovely relationship until one day one of them (I will call her Samantha) was promoted and simply expected her colleague (Billy) to tow the party line when she wanted to implement a new process.

It wasn't a big deal... until it was.

Now obviously the new working relationship required an honest conversation around the blurred boundaries of this new situation (which hadn't quite worked out when I came onboard) and there was clearly some fog and lack of clarity what that looked like. However the crunch came with the unsaid *expectation* that Billy would just fall in line with Samantha's big plans and that would be that.

And when he didn't, that disappointment and disbelief consumed her. She was enraged by his betrayal and couldn't find a conciliatory way to discuss it without losing her cool.

So, this is an interesting lesson and I've heard many similar stories in family businesses where disagreements have escalated to the point it has split families down the middle. And that is tragic.

I will discuss boundaries and healthy relationships in Chapter 10 but for now let me leave you with this thought. Business is always Personal.

Assumptions Around No Message

I recently ran a training session with a senior leadership team and one topic that we discussed was the contentious message of ... 'no message'

Complete radio silence. Nothing.

This is one of my pet hates. Last year I was preparing for a training session and as I am a little OCD I check and double check what I need in advance. I don't like surprises, particularly around technology!

So, a week before the training, I sent an email to the manager who had organized the workshop outlining my requirements and asking her to confirm that everything was ok.

I heard nothing back.

I knew her daughter had been unwell, so I left it a few days before contacting her again with a polite check in email.

Still no response.

I had no option but to show up and kept my fingers crossed that all my requests were in place with a back-up plan if they weren't.

When I arrived, she greeted me with a big smile (making no reference to my emails) but made a grand gesture to show me that all my requirements had been taken care of. I didn't mention her lack of response but I did make a note to add it into my slide deck for future leadership training to illustrate how the message of no message can create unnecessary anxiety and worry.

Now of course this was a 'client / supplier' relationship and the implications and meaning for me will be a different dynamic to a manager / employee or business owner / team member who might experience a communication scarcity.

For example, when you fail to reply to an email or message that you were sent over a week ago, regardless of the content or who it was from. Or you ignore personal emails requesting time off yet happily respond to all work emails. And then there are those situations when *you* assumed someone else cc'd in the correspondence had taken care of it. And finally the promise you made to come back with an answer but never follow up on it (like the example from the mediation in Chapter 3).

The ridiculous thing is that you probably have the answer to all the requests you receive or *assume* an email doesn't warrant a reply. Or you may expect that your team member should know the outcome through telepathy. But if you don't communicate clearly and in a timely manner, don't be surprised if you face a stream of backlash and unwelcome responses.

Affirmative Assumptions

What happens when one of your team members is expecting to hear *yes* and what they hear instead is *no*.

As I mentioned in Chapter 4, for *People Pleasers* this can be a challenging word. But sometimes it is a necessity and I have seen the uproar caused when it has been assumed the answer will be a big thumbs up!

This might be a request for time off or changes to flexible or agile working. They may ask to swap days in the office to suit them (but not you) and suddenly it can become a personal vendetta against you. Even though the reasons for declining will be valid, they won't necessarily be heard or understood. The news might not just be disappointing but also shocking. And that is often where rebellion and dissidence take shape.

So, these situations need to be managed with both confidence and kid gloves. A huge part of the success of these difficult events is apportioned to your relationships with your teams which is often overlooked and underestimated. Fear not however, because I will be dedicating a sizeable chunk to this very point in the following pages.

Expectations. This is How it Should be Done!

I was recently chatting with a colleague about her daughter's return home following a year abroad. The move back to the family abode was a temporary one until she settled into a new apartment. My colleague however was concerned about navigating the dynamics of the homecoming and as we chatted it through, it became clear there was more to this than I originally thought.

The issue related to her daughter's approach to her work ethos. While she was living abroad, she worked from her bedroom, lolling about in her tracksuit, relaxed and chilled, which my colleague assumed must *surely* impact her daughter's productivity and attitude.

The expectation was that she *should* be showered and *properly* dressed, sitting downstairs at her desk, bright eyed and bushy tailed ready to start the day at 9:00 am. Because that is the principle my colleague adhered to.

And there was the essence of the problem. That word *should!* That expectation that because that was her parent's attitude to a correct work ethic, that's what they expected her to follow too.

And here was where I sensed potential conflict brewing. That misalignment of values creating conflicting expectations.

I asked if her daughter performed well in her current role. Absolutely she proudly agreed. Did her work conduct present a problem for her current employer? Not as far as they knew, she replied. Was she seeking financial support from her parents on her return? No she responded.

So why, I asked, was it so jarring for them? Why were they so fixated that she *should* follow her parent's suit because as far as I could understand, this clash of expectations was the source of the trouble?

I respect the fact some people might take the view...*My Home, My Rules*. But what's interesting is if you want to live in harmony, you have a choice.

You either explore and acknowledge *your* triggers around these differences and learn to accept them .... Or live (and work) together in discord.

If we were to examine what underpins our belief systems using the example I have just shared above, I suggest there are several components that oppose our own expectations of a situation.

1. **Our Values**: They dictate what's important to us and shape our world view, our principles in life and how we chose to live it. Remember these are *our values*, no-one elses.

2. **Our Learning style**: The expectation that we all learn and absorb information the same way is incorrect as I illustrated above in the example with the manger and her assistant. We don't. Our skills are learned based on the process our brain likes to decipher information using the VARK model. We might be a Visual, Auditory, Reading / Writing or Kinaesthetic learner. I for example have far greater success remembering even a basic shopping list if I visualise the items. But if they were dictated to me as a verbal list... no chance!

3. **Our Environment**: This is an awareness of our surroundings and whether we work better in a quiet,

noisy, bustling, formal, creative, or busy space. Do we for example find inspiration in the office bouncing impromptu ideas off colleagues or sitting in a coffee shop watching the world go by. Or does the peace and quiet, informality and relaxed state of our bedroom calm, motivate and bring out our best work. This is a good question not just for my colleague to mull over but for anyone expecting their teams or colleagues to work in the same vein as they do.

I hope by now you have a good insight into the many factors that give rise to conflict and that if unchecked can necessitate some very challenging conversations. So let's now move onto Part 2. Cure... and explore how to manage and master those interactions to ensure they are as successful as possible.

Exploratory and Journaling Questions:

1. When and where have you made an assumption that created a problem with your teams or colleagues?
2. Do you make assumptions around the abilities of your teams?
3. Does your ambiguous communication lead to confusion?
4. Have you encountered issues in the workplace with family and friends based on assumptions around your relationships?
5. What action will you now take to avoid assumptions?

PART II
CURE

"The Best Cure for the Body is a Quiet Mind"

— *NAPOLEON BONAPARTE*

6

IT ALL STARTS WITH YOU!

> "Whether you think you can or you can't you're right."
>
> — HENRY FORD

In my opinion, one of the fundamental reasons why a conversation gets off on the wrong footing is not just the way we conduct it but the way we approach it. The way we think about it. How we feel about it. Our anticipation of what may or may not occur. Our responses. Our mindset towards it and the preparation for it both emotionally and physically.

As I mentioned in Chapter 1, there are several explanations why we find ourselves tongue tied, stuck, triggered or too complacent. Equally, there are reasons why we chose to kick the can down the road and do *anything* other than engage in a difficult dialogue.

It starts with awareness of your feelings towards the impending conversation.

Facing the Fear

Fear is a very powerful force. And it can show up in so many guises.

- Fear that the conversation didn't go to plan last time so won't this time.
- Fear of pushback.
- Fear of confrontation.
- Fear of being judged by colleagues.
- Fear of speaking up.
- Fear of not being heard.
- Fear of becoming unpopular.
- Fear of damaging relationships.
- Fear of losing control of the conversation.
- Fear of looking inept and incompetent through poor articulation.

It activates our cortisol levels invoking a physiological response. It's a visceral reaction and for everyone it manifests in a different point in our body.

Some people experience a dry mouth, a ferociously pounding headache, sweaty palms and that nauseating churn in our stomach... hence the expression feeling sick to the stomach!

I always feel it as a tightness in my chest.... And yes, I still do have difficult conversations despite my expertise!

This is our Fight, Flight and Freeze response kicking in to protect us from potential danger. Maybe not physical danger but emotional danger! For example, the threat of judgement, ruin, reputational damage, broken relationships.

Fight: Our defences are up as we prepare for battle! Remember the Warrior Archetype?

Flight: Run! Avoid or meander around the conversation altogether which feels much safer.

Freeze: Silence prevails, and we lose our voice and do nothing.

In prehistoric days when we were being chased by wild animals, this was a very useful safety mechanism. Today, in our day-to-day work-life and business interactions… not so much!

So first and foremost, we need to identify what is provoking that debilitating fear and how to tame it.

This is where reflection comes into play. Quite simply, what has happened in the past that you're afraid will happen again? Because this is what our brain recalls and tries to avoid from re-occurring. It's an uneasy state we don't like sitting in.

It might bring up memories of uncomfortable moments when a feedback conversation hit a wall, or we faced a confrontational client who we couldn't appease. Or we appeared incompetent in front of our teams, escalating a disagreement between them rather than diffusing it. Or we recollect a time when we bumbled our way through a meeting with our boss or colleagues, sweating under the spotlight, acutely aware of the absence of the requested answers or facts.

In order to manage it more expertly next time, we need to pinpoint the exact event that caused us such distress. This is the first step towards a new and more helpful approach for future conversations. Because you can't fix it until you know what the problem is.

A good way to start this process is to journal (unless of course you know with certainty what's really going on). I would recommend brain dump your thoughts onto paper and watch what unfolds. Sometimes the fear is hidden so deep in our unconscious that it isn't until we allow it to free flow onto paper that it lifts the fog and we have some clarity on our real worries. Alternatively, talk it through with a trusted friend or family member and see what emerges.

Identify the fear before you search for the remedy to cure it.

Decluttering your Mind

Ever since I was a child, I remember my father as an avid bridge player. Two or three times a week he could be found at his local club as well as hosting a regular Monday night game at home.

A few months ago, we were chatting at dinner, and he casually mentioned he had recently won another tournament!

While at age 87, this was a great achievement in itself (and a fairly usual occurrence), he then modestly slipped into the conversation that he'd come 7th out of 25,000 nationally!

Well, I was blown away!

We spent some time discussing and exploring the secret to his success and he shared that he believed his game was stronger now than ever before.

Apart from endless years of experience contributing to his success, what fascinated me the most was one point he made that as he's now retired with less clutter and 'work worries' in his mind, he's able to have razor sharp focus with few distractions when he plays.

And this was so interesting because I believe it can be applied to all the unhelpful minds chatter we are preoccupied with during a conflict or challenging conversations. Our head is often full of 'distractions' as we ruminate on the impending and current conversation.

We anticipate how the person might respond or we play out the *'what ifs'* of potential pushback and fill our mind with negative self-talk. Or we spend our time entertaining our thoughts with assumptions about *their* response.

Yet all this creates is a vortex of confusion playing with our ability to concentrate.

We forget what we want to say. We lose focus, we struggle to articulate ourselves well. We react rather than respond. We become derailed.

My suggestion is to take a leaf out of my very impressive 87-year-old dad's book and declutter your mind first using one (or all) of the following techniques.

Preparing Yourself – Getting into the Zone

There are many sports that follow a formulaic process and rituals in their preparation, to get the competitors into *'the zone'*. In rugby the *All Blacks* perform the menacing 'Haka'. In Sumo wrestling, the *Rikishi* (Wrestlers) carry out a ritual of throwing salt, stamping their feet, and slapping themselves which is all part of the customary ceremony.

The point is these rituals help focus their mindset and prepare them for the competition ahead. And similarly, you need to create your own practises to prepare yourself for your difficult conversations. To get into the right state of mind and zone so you are grounded, focused and laser sharp.

So, how do you do that?

When *that* conversation is looming, it's likely you will be in one of several states. Anxious, angry, afraid, nervous, stressed, edgy. Your priority is to find a way to shift into a more helpful mindset; from angry to calm or from anxious to confident. However, in order to do that, it's essential to first acknowledge your current state and then identify what a more empowering one looks like.

And here is how I worked out how to do that!

Several years ago, I set out for my daily morning walk. The sun was shining. All seemed well in my world.

I put my headphones in and searched for one of my favourite podcasts.

Off I went.

About five minutes into my walk, I realised that I was not enjoying the episode. In fact, it was really irritating me.

So, I quickly scrolled through my podcast library and switched to another show which always inspired and motivated me.

Again, after listening for several minutes... I turned it off. It just wasn't hitting the spot and by now I was very jittery. I knew I had to pull myself together with a day ahead that needed my focus and attention on point.

So, I switched to my Apple playlist. Shuffling through it aimlessly, I continued to flick through song after song that failed to do anything other than frustrate me further.

Until I struck gold!

Boom! I had found my perfect tune!

Suddenly there I was skipping down the street feeling revitalized, motivated and much happier.

How simple was that?

And that's when I discovered the power of music to change

my emotional state and a ritual I follow whenever I have a situation on the horizon that requires a shift in focus and energy.

Why don't you try it?

Search through your playlists, Apple Music or anywhere you store your music. Pick three of your *absolute favourite* songs. This should be music that you can't help but sing, hum or even dance along to whenever you hear it. Songs that energise you and leave you feeling empowered, invincible, confident, ready to face whatever challenges lie ahead.

These are the tunes you will tap into when you feel panicky, nervous, or apprehensive. When you hear that inner critic and mind chatter telling you to back away. Think of them as your musical *pep talk* and confidence booster, inspiring you and telling you... you've got this!

Then choose three more that bring you calm and serenity when you feel edgy, stressed, or angry. These will feature as your 'go to' tracks to soothe your soul and quieten your inner rage.

Keep a note of them somewhere handy and memorable so that if you get caught off guard, you can easily access them.

Mindset Matters – Knowing your State

I am unashamedly a big Tom Cruise fan.

One of my all-time favourite films is the original Top Gun movie .... No, it's not just because he's very easy on the eye ... although that is a big win for me!

There is a wonderful scene near the beginning where he straddles his Kawasaki bike and rides at breakneck speed alongside the airstrip of the Top Gun School watching the F16s taking off and landing. Wind in his hair, a knowing smile, feeling exhilarated, pure joy, freedom and at peace. He has found *'his happy place'*.

This is his sweet spot. A place and moment that no doubt would be imprinted in his memory bank. (I know it's not real life but just play along with me here!)

What is the relevance of this you might be thinking?

Well, here's the point.

Everyone needs one of these memories that take you to another place, time, or zone. A place to visit before a challenging conversation. Like music, a visual memory can have the same overwhelmingly powerful effect on your emotional state and being.

A place to soothe your soul. To lift your mood, shift your mindset and transport you out of your current state to a place that brings you confidence, courage, and strength.

Like your three songs, I suggest you make a mental and written note of your *happy place* or memory to conjure up when need be.

While both music and visual memories are great mood shifters to prepare yourself for a difficult conversation, so are all the following: Taking yourself off for a walk in the woods or along a deserted beach, listening to an inspiring podcast, riding *your* Kawasaki bike along the open road, running for miles through the countryside, meditating, a swim in the ocean or your local pool. Equally, if you don't have time or opportunity to do any of these activities, a quick walk around the block will do just as well.

The point is to do *anything* that works for you that will change your energy and state.

Focus on the Goal

What is your intention or goal for the conversation? What do you hope to achieve? This is critical, otherwise you will go around and around in circles without any clear focus and waste your energy and breath on a dialogue with no specific outcome.

If it's a performance conversation with one of your teams, are you looking for increased output, a change in behaviour or attitude or to raise awareness of a problem?

With a colleague, are you hoping for an apology or explanation? With your own boss, are you seeking more support or direction? With a client, do you want understanding or to set some firm boundaries?

Whichever it is, be clear from the get-go and use this as a reference point if the conversation veers off track.

Reframe the Conversation

Many people view difficult conversations as a negative. I personally believe, that if they are managed competently, they are an opportunity for change and not challenge. So the way you think about them can influence the way they pan out.

If you believe you are going into battle, fighting for survival rather than seeking a solution or a collaborative outcome, you may find the conversation less than fruitful. If however, you consider it a chance to clear the air and move forward to a conciliatory place, I am certain you will enjoy a more successful result.

A technique we often use in both mediation and coaching is future visioning a positive outcome. This is a very powerful practise.

Let me explain why.

*Every thought or visualisation we have evokes **an emotion**.* So if we believe and visualise the conversation will be smooth without any hiccups, it will elicit confidence.

*Every **emotion** sparks a drive to take action.* And if we feel confident, we will be more inspired to be bolder and more assertive in our communication. We might push ourselves and the conversation that little bit further.

*And every **action** creates a result.* If we are more assertive the chances, are we will have a more promising conversation achieving our intended goal and a successful conclusion.

As Henry Ford, the founder of The Ford Motor Company advocated... "Whether you think you can or can't, you're right", meaning that if you view the conversation as being difficult, it probably will be. But if you believe you will breeze through it effortlessly, you will!

Preparation

From a very young age we are encouraged to prepare for key events in life like exams, crucial meetings and presentations. In fact anything significant that requires focus, skill and aptitude. And there is a good reason for this. It gives us confidence and poise. Without it we become easily derailed and distracted. Not all of us are adept at *winging it*!

As I mentioned earlier, our *Fight, Flight, Freeze* response has a wonderful way of clouding our memory when we need to rely on it the most or when we strive to find the right words in the moment.

So, preparing for these conversations is equally essential. However this doesn't just relate to the content, but also formulating answers for possible pushback you might anticipate or objections you might encounter. Being ready for those *'what if'* moments. This certainty and knowledge that you have an immediate solution at your fingertips will help to pacify the creeping fear.

And once you have those responses ready, then rehearse those variables so that when the conversation hits a roadblock, you are well versed and confident in your retort. Forewarned is forearmed.

Take a little time in advance of the conversation to scribble a few written notes or compose memory joggers on your phone. Craft bullet points or mind-map it. Whatever it takes to give you the confidence to communicate eloquently.

Now I appreciate that you can't anticipate all eventualities and may be blindsided by some reactions. But don't let that knock you off track. Using the above techniques will support you to stay grounded, calm and present.

The Approach

A careless or ill-considered start to any challenging conversation will often have a disastrous outcome. Even the invitation to it should be well planned to avoid provocation.

The following suggestions might be less activating.

"Could we schedule some time in the diary to chat something through?"

"There's something on my mind I'd love to talk to you about. When works for you?"

In this example, you are paving the way and setting the tone for what lies ahead. A gentle, honest, and calm conversation. Although it is clear there is an agenda, it's not as provocative as this hostile approach ... "We need to talk!"

Once face to face, consider how you initiate the conversation. Launch in like a bull in a china shop and it's unlikely to get off on the right footing.

Open too insipidly and you will have lost them at hello or they will walk all over you.

I often present this in training as an analogy of a plane coming into land. The approach must be managed skilfully, meticulously, cautiously and with careful consideration otherwise, the conversation, like the plane, may well crash and burn!

Try out a few options in private to see how they *land* with you. Something like this might work well with a colleague you disagree with.

"Thank you for agreeing to meet with me. I wanted to share my thoughts with you about the meeting yesterday and would welcome yours too".

If it's a performance issue with one of your teams.

"I would be interested to understand what happened so we can work together to prevent the same mistake occurring again".

Don't forget that our approach isn't confined to just our words. It also relates to our non-verbal communication... body language, our tone of voice, how we show up and the *Communication Baggage* we carry. If they are misaligned with our words, whatever we are saying will lose its' impact and effect.

It's the whole package that needs to be in harmony.

Presence and Confidence

In order to influence, command authority and build trust, you need to have presence. And in all the difficult conversations I have ever engaged in, these attributes are key.

Presence and confidence are intrinsically linked.

If you are familiar with the work of social psychologist Amy Cuddy, you will appreciate why.

A professor and researcher at Harvard Business School and bestselling author, she studies the impact of non-verbal behaviour in high stakes situations.

She is well known for her study of 'Power Posing' which is a technique associated to mentally empower us to feel confident in stressful situations when we feel anything but assertive. Her studies have shown how these positive stances where we mimic powerful body language can boost feelings of self-assurance leading to a greater opportunity for success.

So, what is 'Power Posing'?

I call it *confidence trickery*. Power Posing is adopting wide open postures or positions that appear to take up a vast expanse of space. The *Wonder Woman* pose is a good example where you stand with your feet apart, your hands on your hip and your chin tilted upwards. Cuddy suggests you assume a 'Power Pose' for a few minutes before any event where your confidence is low. This is something you might like to do in private though to avoid strange looks from passers-by!

In her book '**Presence'**, she shares the story of a study she conducted where candidates were informed, they were participating in a mock job interview. Half the participants were told to adopt a High 'Power Pose' (open stance) for a few minutes before the interview and the remaining half to assume a Low 'Power Pose' (closed stance). They were judged by interviewers on several different criteria, one of which was their non-verbal presence. Those who adopted the high 'Power Pose' scored significantly better and interviewers cited they were *significantly* more likely to be hired for the mock job based on their observations.

So, what is the relevance of this?

When we need to bring our boldest self to a difficult conversation, sometimes our body language gives us away. What comes out of our mouth might sound impressive and confident but one look at the non-verbal cues might inform otherwise.

To illustrate this further, I wonder if you have ever considered your body positioning when you're happy or sad?

Try this exercise.

Think of a time when you received some great news. Winning an award, winning a new client, winning a race. A natural action is to *fist pump* the air, or throw both arms up in a 'V' or victory pose above your head as you cross the finish line. It's an open stance indicating joy and confidence.

Now think of the same exciting event and imagine taking that final step through the finishing tape to cheering crowds or standing on the podium accepting your trophy, hunched forwards, head bowed, focused downwards, in an inward *closed* stance.

I'm certain it would feel incongruent with the euphoric words you are expressing.

Therefore, I believe 'Power Posing' can be an empowering tool before an important conversation when your confidence is waning. This will support you to exude authority, command respect and to show up as the experienced and knowledgeable leader you are.... Even if you don't feel like it.

Self-Reflection and Self Awareness

How do you want to be remembered? As a kind, generous, supportive, thoughtful, and caring leader or business owner?

I mean .... who wouldn't?

Sometimes though, we aren't aware of our contribution to a

problem or how our behaviour is impacting others. And that requires a little self-awareness.

I have facilitated countless mediations over the years where a department head has stepped in to manage teams while looking for a replacement middle manager. Knowing this was a temporary role they might not have paid it the attention it deserves particularly if other more pressing issues might have taken priority. They allowed behavioural or performance issues to fall by the wayside because they knew someone else might pick this up at a later date.

This becomes problematic when the new enthusiastic manager steps into the role to do what they were hired to do. To manage their teams. However the moment they attempt to address issues and attitude, stamp out the behaviour or make unpopular changes, they are descended upon, blamed, and accused of bullying and micromanaging.... And unfortunately, that's down to the Leader's apathy or reluctance to get involved previously.

And this is where some self-reflection and awareness are necessary and an opportunity to review your role in this messy situation.

What about performance management. If you're honest, have you made yourself as available and accessible as you could have been if your teams' productivity was flagging? Could you have encouraged them more and assisted further? Were you as supportive as possible or could you have organised additional training where there were gaps or weaknesses in their abilities?

Years ago, in my former PR career. I had a boss who had her own 'special' communication style. She could often be heard calling people 'f***ing d***heads' around the Agency if they made a mistake.

Which wasn't very nice or respectful.

But here's the interesting thing. She was a brilliant MD and I learnt so much from her.

But thirty-five odd years later. This is my lasting impression. This is what defined her.

Not the times when she ordered pizza for the whole department when we were working late on a pitch.

Nor when she rewarded and recognised people in the company monthly meetings who had excelled that month.

Nor the occasions people had been promoted and she took the time to share why.

But for all the good, kind, and inspirational things she did, she let herself down the way she spoke to us. That's my lasting memory.

And that's a shame.

Yet I'm not convinced she ever stopped to evaluate the impact of her behaviour. She had a big heart but a big mouth too!

Business is about relationships and once a line is crossed, the damage is done and it's harder (although not impossible) to repair. However as I trust you are now realizing, it's so much easier to prevent it in the first place. With a little self-awareness and tweaks to your communication style!

Managing Triggers

I will explore *why* we are triggered in chapter 7 but for now I would like to focus on managing those moments with a little more finesse! The words you speak can't be unspoken. The way you react is how you will be defined and remembered. This was illustrated in the example above.

The second you recognize your reaction, do one thing and one thing only.

Press the pause button.

I appreciate this is probably the last thing you want to do but believe me it is the safest choice!

If you are incensed about an email. Stop. Count to ten. Close your computer or phone. It never works out well for keyboard warriors! Do *anything* except reply to that message when you are in that state. Grab a coffee, go for a walk around the block, put the kettle on, talk to a friend, colleague, or partner, listen to some music, meditate, journal, pour a glass of wine. And breathe...

Give yourself some bandwidth to reflect and review. I personally always try and wait until the following day before replying in these circumstances. That space and a good night's sleep brings perspective and clarity. I appreciate however the luxury of time is not always on our side.

I ask myself some honest questions. Am I over-reacting? Or is my response fair and justified (at least in my books!)

I revisit the email or message. Is it as bad as I originally thought? If not, I park it and move on, grateful that I didn't escalate this to full blown combat.

If you try all the above and it's still bothering you, I suggest where possible to discuss the issue face to face, using all the tools from this chapter to prepare yourself.

As the conversation plays out and you start to engage in verbal ping pong, acknowledge this and bring your focus back round to your goal for the conversation.

If you are triggered in a meeting, use the same methodology. Do not react in the moment. Pause, Excuse yourself, take five and manage your mindset. You might just save your relationships.

Remember every action sparks a reaction. The *only* thing you can control is your own response so be mindful of this as it will dictate how the conversation pans out.

You will discover more useful tools and techniques in Chapter 7 that will support you further but for now, never *ever* respond in your triggered state!

So, this brings us to the end of this chapter but if you take nothing else from the content, I would like to offer you a helpful little acronym to assist you in those moments when you need a quick prop. Use a M.A.P.

M:Manage your **Mindset**

A:Be clear about what you want to **Achieve**

P:Prepare yourself as well as the conversation

Exploratory and Journaling Questions:

1. What would your 6 six '*go to*' songs be to shift your mindset?
2. Do you have a *happy place*? If not, take some time to search for it. You'll know when you have found it!
3. What *Power Pose* would you adopt to feel more empowered?
4. Do you believe you are self-aware or self-reflect?
5. If not, what small things could you start to do to change that?

7
TOOLS, TIPS AND TECHNIQUES

"Honesty, Courage and Authenticity are a Pipeline for Connection rather than a barrier to Communication."

— NICOLE POSNER

Now that we have explored how to prepare yourself for those challenging dialogues, I would like to offer you what I consider the key ingredients for successful leadership communication.

I am a big fan of acronyms as a memory tool so if you're not, I apologise now as I have included several in this chapter!

The Influence of Curiosity

You may be familiar with the expression *Curiosity killed the cat*, however in your challenging interactions, it is a life saver.

Curiosity, when used with the right intention, is one of the most powerful tools to initiate change without challenge, deflect anger and encourage investment into ideas and processes without employing strong arm tactics.

Here are a few examples where it can prove victorious if the right questions are proposed.

The key is to invite opinions rather than impose views.

Introducing change and new systems for example can often be met with resistance. Asking your team members for their input into a new idea can be more rewarding than you anticipate. If they believe they have made a valuable contribution to something of enormous importance to the business, they will be more invested in it and consequently more committed to it. And as a bonus, new perspective brings new vision so some innovative ideas may even emerge too!

Your teams are often closer to problems than you are, so seeking their contribution and inviting their thoughts can bring a new dimension into the problem solving process too.

Another effective use of curiosity is investigating *why* mistakes have been made. Gently probing your teams to consider why they think the task went off course or didn't go to plan is a much more effective management tool than chastising them. The benefit here is that this process will attract an element of reflection and awareness.

What about dead-end conversations when you have opposing ideas to your colleagues and they emphatically believe theirs are the best ... yet you don't. As opposed to shutting them down and risking an ugly contretemps, you could use curiosity to explore more possibilities.

Using the *traffic light system* explained later in this chapter, listen first, echo back what you have heard and when you have their attention, suggest the following:

"How can we improve on this / embellish it / expand it?"

In this instance, you are giving it some airtime, but equally not accepting it in its present form which is far from perfect.

To take this concept a step further, I have designed a helpful acronym and framework to employ when managing performance, resistance, and tension in your teams.... *Curious* and here is how it works.

Clarify, **U**nderstand, **R**eframe, **I**nvestigate, **O**bserve, **U**nearth, **S**upport

Clarify: We all know what assumptions are the mother of! Never end a conversation without clarity around responsibilities of actions and timelines.

Understand: A frequent mistake inexperienced managers or *Freshers* make is not taking the time to explore *why* a team member's performance is slacking. Instead they manage the outcome of it, the missed deadline, the unmet targets, or sloppy errors which means the problems will continue to happen until the source of it is identified and addressed.

Reframe: Faced with resistance to a new process or change, it's not unusual for team members to say, "I can't do that!" A better reframe of this declaration would be to add a positive end to the sentence... "I can't do this *yet*".

Investigate: Taking issues at face value or taking sides is dangerous. You can't make a judgement until you are in possession of all the facts. While the *Freshers* for example might jump in with a quick solution and view this as an opportunity to impress their boss or swiftly knock the problem on its head, that impatience could possibly be their downfall if they don't take the time to investigate what's really going on.

Observe: What behaviours and reactions do you observe? Be mindful of what isn't being verbalised. Look at their body language. As you will now know, that will be revealing too.

Unearth: Poor behaviours and attitude are always propelled by an underlying driver. I will focus more on this in Chapter 10 however for now I think it is sufficient to say that it's vital to dig deep and unearth what's sitting underneath the surface issues. It's not always what it first appears to be.

Support: Once you have understood, explored, and investigated, what support can you offer having gathered all the facts?

There's a Time and a Place

As I have alluded to in previous chapters, we are what we bring to the table. It's vital to schedule the conversation when *you* have time for it. Don't squeeze it in just before a presentation when your focus will be elsewhere. Or when you are rushing from one meeting to the next and your energy might be depleted. You may of course be carrying some hefty *Communication Baggage* from your last encounter too!

If it's an impromptu conversation that must happen immediately, take a minute or two and pause before you begin, check in with yourself about your state, energy, and mindset and if you have the opportunity, plug in your earphones, and listen to one of your six choice tunes.

As for the location of your conversation, I recommend you take it outside... no I don't mean squaring up to your colleague and proposing a round in the boxing ring!

If it's a conversation with a colleague or a team member, find somewhere neutral you both feel on equal footing and comfortable, away from prying eyes and ears. Go for a coffee or anywhere that creates space away from your working environment. The change of scenery can often generate a positive change in atmosphere and diffuse tension. This is of course assuming it's not a virtual meeting or a phone call.

The Importance of Relationships

I cannot emphasise enough the importance of relationship building with your teams as well as clients and colleagues. Let me explain.

When you hit a roadblock or are faced with a tough conversation, it is so much easier to navigate if you share good rapport and genuine connection. I'm referring to real, authentic relationships where honesty is appreciated, not resented.

Have you ever received unsolicited advice from a stranger which really niggles you? Yet you hear the exact same suggestions from a trusted friend or colleague who you like and gratefully accept it with open arms.

That's down to your relationships and knowing the latter advice is coming from a place of integrity and care with no ulterior motive.

So how do you nurture relationships with your teams?

I recommend you invest some time getting to know your people. I'm not referring to their abilities or strengths and weaknesses. I mean really understanding who they are. Their likes and dislikes. Identifying their motivators and drivers.

Enquire about their life outside the workplace. Do you know their birthdays? Are they married, in a relationship or single? Do they have children and if so, how many? What are their names and ages? Which football team do they support? What are their hobbies, favourite foods, or TV shows.

These are the things that connect and bring people together. Particularly if you share some common interests. The purpose is not to pry or stick your nose into their private life. If this process is natural and intuitive it won't appear creepy, odd or intrusive.

These might be facts you discover during those *water cooler moments*, making a cup of tea in the office kitchen or queueing for a coffee at Starbucks. Note and remember them so that when you have your next check in call or chat, you can ask how their son's football match went or if their daughter had received her exam grades back. Or on their birthday, you could make a point of writing a card or buying a small cake.

If your team member's mother tongue is a foreign language, you could learn their native greetings, so they feel included in the daily round of morning acknowledgments. Or take an interest in their culture and incorporate one of their traditions such as the Japanese etiquette of bowing.

All these small gestures may appear insignificant (and maybe silly to you) but to your teams, it illustrates that you are interested in them and value them. It will motivate and drive them and during times of pressure and stress, you will reap the rewards by their loyalty and support in return.

When the proverbial s**t *hits the fan* or you are called upon to step up to address a problem, they will believe you are championing them from a place of kindness and integrity not malice or malintent. And that's how trust is built.

"I Hope You're Well"

Not a lot surprises me... however last year I was blown away by a comment made by one party in a mediation, which, on reflection, was actually very sad. She shared how she had been 'overjoyed' by an email sent by her boss who was the other party in the mediation, sitting opposite her.

The first line of the email read... "Hi X, I hope you're well?".

I was confused!

"That's good? Right?" I asked.

"Yes", she enthusiastically replied. "I didn't care what the rest of the email said. I was just so happy she'd cared enough to bother asking how I was!"

"Doesn't she usually?" I enquired.

"No, never". She quipped back.

Her boss flushed. And then flustered, shared she didn't have time for *'niceties'* in her emails. She was so busy. She continued that no-one else in her team was offended by her communication style. They just accepted it! Aha!! And there it was!

The source of the problem.

The assumption that *everyone* was in fact ok with her tone and *happy* to receive information in her curt and blunt manner.

Had she stopped to reflect or even ask? I think not.

She hadn't devoted any time or effort to discover who her team members were, what made them tick and what they valued... as was evident with this relationship.

Had she made this small investment, I doubt we would have been sitting in that mediation.

Four words used more frequently "I hope you're well..." could have changed the trajectory of the preceding three years for them and their very fractured and toxic relationship.

Remember your teams are your most valuable asset, so take the time to demonstrate them that they are valued!

The Power of Listening

If I was asked my top five tips for better communication, listening would be one of them. I believe it is a superpower. Honing your listening skills is an art worth mastering.

I appreciate it is hard to sit quietly and listen, particularly if you don't necessarily agree with what you are hearing, or your mind is full of a million distracting thoughts taking your focus away from the conversation. It takes courage, stamina, and patience.

But a great leader does just that.

- It is a chance to pause and evaluate what's being said.
- It is an opportunity to understand and be curious.
- It prevents assumptions that can lead to a host of costly challenges.
- It gives you time to consider what strategies to employ to deflect anger.
- It shows you respect others' views even if you don't share them.
- It gives you the opportunity to see the situation from another perspective.
- It illustrates you value other opinions rather than being dismissive of them.
- It diffuses tension and brings calm to a heated discussion.

- It encourages others to open up and speak freely.
- It comforts and pacifies those in pain.
- It is a powerful aid to encourage a two-way dialogue when a confrontational conversation reaches stalemate.
- It shows respect.

I actually thought I was a good listener until I attended my initial mediation training quite a few years ago. We commenced day one with an exercise on listening skills.

Paired up with our neighbour, we spent two minutes introducing ourselves to each other and then were asked, one by one, to introduce our neighbour to the group. I was last and by the time it was my turn, I was a little jittery and nervous.

Enthusiastically, I shared what I remembered about my partner, Paul, and was quite pleased with my recollection and happy I got through it without forgetting any key points.

At the end, he smiled and thanked me but said little more to me until the morning break. I didn't think too much about it until he coyly mentioned over coffee that most of the information I recalled was correct ... except his name! I'd got it wrong! It was Peter!

I was so embarrassed. But actually, this wasn't about me or my bruised ego. It was the impact of the experience on him.

Names are funny things. We carry them like a trophy. We are protective of them. We wear them like a badge. Not listening to Peter's name made him feel unrecognised and invalidated. When this happens in the workplace, your teams will disengage and disconnect, and this is when relationships start to fall apart.

So, if you want to bring out the best in your teams, listen to them, demonstrate they are valued ... or you might just lose them at hello!

Listening to diffuse conflict is a secret weapon!

Let's take an example where you and a colleague have come to blows over a difference of opinion. The last thing you care to do when you are angry is to listen to them. The red mist falls, you are both engaged in verbal ping pong, focusing on delivering the next jibe.

However, this will do nothing except incite your sparring partner further and escalate the problem. It's a vicious cycle. The result? No-one *hears* anything except the sound of their own voice and the conversation hits a brick wall.

It's human desire to be acknowledged and heard, yet when we are not, we become frustrated and more indignant. We dig our heels in and refuse to budge. Our words are rolling off the tip of our tongue before our partner has finished their sentence.

Are you familiar with the expression, two ears and one mouth? The meaning behind it is we should listen more and talk less.

We all listen at different levels depending on the circumstances, our concentration and focus, our environment and our interest in the conversation! Yet to listen well, we need to be fully present.

As Stephen Covey advocates in his brilliant book 7 *Habits of Highly Effective People*:

"Seek first to understand, then to be understood."

So, I have devised a process that I refer to as the *traffic light system* to overcome this obstacle. It requires a willingness from one person to *listen first*. If this sounds too abhorrent to you, concentrate on your goal for the conversation which is ultimately more important than the immediate discomfort or angst of *appearing* to give in. Because this is a false perception that if you listen quietly and without interruption, you are therefore in agreement. This is absolutely not true.

Red: This is a *no-go* zone. Don't engage in a dialogue until you have listened to your conversational partner first. Why? Because the power of feeling heard is magical. It reduces tension and brings calm and the process of *offloading* is cathartic meaning once they have *vomited* up all their thoughts, they will be better placed to hear yours.

Amber: Echo back what you heard in your own words. This is the *key*. However, a word of caution. Do so without *poking the bear*, judging, adding a sarcastic jibe or throwing in your two pennies worth. This illustrates *you* have heard and acknowledged *them* which is a powerful vehicle to move the conversation forward. A phrase such as..." So, what you are saying is..." Or "What I have understood is ...". You want to elicit an affirmation. A confirmation. A response of "Yes! Exactly!"

Green: You might observe a change in their non-verbal cues or notice less rigidity and tension in the stance or posture. This is a good indication they are willing to listen back. Start with "I hear you" and then continue with your points. I am sure you will be surprised by the change in attitude.

This process encourages a two-way dialogue rather than a one-way rant!

A great illustration of the power of listening was displayed at the start of a mediation several years ago.

During the individual session with one of the parties, I watched the body language of the man opposite me with curiosity. He sat tight lipped and appeared very frosty. His arms were crossed defensively across his body as he gripped his satchel firmly to his chest. All signs indicated he had no desire to be talking to me. He was polite but resistant. It was hard to draw information from him. He was a tough nut to crack. I gently probed, I cautiously asked questions and I listened to him.

After about twenty minutes he began to warm up. His body relaxed. His hunched shoulders dropped, he started to open up. We chatted and deconstructed his concerns and issues and I reframed them back to him. Suddenly his whole demeanour changed.

"YES! Exactly!" He shouted excitedly. I got it. I had hit the nail on the head and identified what was at the core of all his troubles. He felt heard and understood and began to trust me which was key.

From that point on the conversation moved forward in a positive and constructive way. He talked freely and we had turned a corner.

He shared that this was the first time anyone had taken the trouble to listen to him and for that he was grateful. In fact, this narrative is something I often experienced over the years, followed by a simple but heartfelt thank you from participants. Feeling heard is both liberating, healing, and calming and that is a big win in the chaos of conflict. So, if you want to herald change without challenge or get to 'Yes' in your difficult conversations, I recommend you hone your listening skills and give your colleagues and team members a really good listening to!

The Value of Values

I'm often asked my views on psychometric testing and personality diagnostic tools. I believe they have a useful place in a handful of circumstances.

I however prefer to use my own assessment tool. Working with what I see in front of me. The whole person. Who they are. What is important to them and exploring their unique view of the world. In short, understanding their values.

Values are the force that make us tick and dictate how we behave and respond. When we strike out, this is a message to back off because something we cherish is being challenged, dismissed or threatened. And we will go to any length to protect it.

This explains why someone might over-react in a situation that to the rest of us may appear petty or irrelevant. This is because the value that was triggered for one individual, may not be at all important to the rest of us.

They are the core reasons relationships breakdown, personalities clash or conflict manifests.

In the moment, we may not be aware what fuelled that spark, but we do know that something pushed our button and created a knee jerk reaction.

A confrontation is just as likely to happen in the Boardroom as it is in on the Shop Floor. In fact, the higher the stakes, the greater the loss which often results in a more volatile outburst or entrenched standpoint. This was the case if you recall, in the example I shared in Chapter 2 with the business owner and her senior leader who were in conflict around hybrid working arrangements.

The business owner was protecting her value of reputation,

while the manager was defending her values of justice and fairness. This underpins the importance of strong relationships with your teams. If you are aware of their values, it will bring you understanding why they react and what's behind it. It's also useful in the hiring and recruitment process to ensure your values, the business values and the candidate's values are all aligned.

Leading with H.E.A.R.T

These are without doubt my five key communication pillars. I believe *at least* one of these traits are embraced in all successful leadership conversations.

Communicating with H.E.A.R.T inspires open and honest dialogue, leads to strong connections, engagement, builds trust and rapport and empowers change without challenge.

So, let's take a look at these five silver bullets!

Humility, **E**mpathy, **A**uthenticity, **R**espect and **T**ransparency

Humility

So, what is humility? Acknowledging you don't have the answers or taking responsibility for what went wrong, apologising or backing down in an argument. While this may feel uncomfortable, this humble approach can open up new pathways to connection. It is a magnet that draws people into your world rather than pushing them away.

A word of caution, if you do express regret or chose to apologise, do so with integrity and leave your ego at the door. An empty apology is worse than no apology. Be clear that you are expressing regret for your actions not how the person feels. For example, don't say you are sorry that your team member or colleague is upset, instead acknowledge regret that you were the cause of the upset.

If you follow football, you might recall the post-match interview with England's manager Gareth Southgate, during the final of the Euros 2020. This was a sterling example of a humble leader.

As a nation here in the UK we were gutted as we watched Marcus Rashford, Jadon Sancho and 19-year-old Bukayo Saka miss the penalty shootout.

Those defining moments will probably haunt them forever.

However, as I watched the post-match commentary with our manager, my spirits were lifted. It was a statement made by our manager.

Southgate shared, without any hesitation that he took responsibility for England's penalty shootout defeat, saying the decisions made were entirely down to him.

There was no blame. No calling out. He was accountable for his decisions and owned them.

I loved his humility and the connection and respect he clearly held for his team.

That is Leadership.

I have worked with so many leaders who have got it wrong and this was a great example of a humble leader who got it right.

Empathy

Empathy is another one of my favourite top tips. Don't confuse it with sympathy because they can evoke very different responses.

It can bridge chasms in relationships and demonstrate support and understanding.

It shows that you *get* it! You recognize and acknowledge where your teams or colleagues are at. It inspires trust when others feel safe enough to open up and it can break down barriers. It illustrates you care; it nurtures connection and engagement, strengthens relationships, and improves team retention.

This story is a great example of what could possibly happen when empathy is missing!

I was recently privy to a very uncomfortable conversation while queueing for my coffee.

And I have to admit, it took every ounce of will power not to offer an opinion or some advice.

Next to me were two men (one of whom I assumed was a manager) engaged in a serious conversation about a missed deadline.

"I'm sinking" one of my fellow coffee lovers shared. "I'm prioritising everything by order of urgency and I know I'm dropping the ball here and there!"

His manager ignored his honest revelation and *unsaid* plea for support.

Instead, he focused on the task that remained unfinished without acknowledging his employee's disheartened and anxious state. His report's face said it all. Deflated, disillusioned, and disappointed he listened to the white noise but appeared to lose engagement or enthusiasm from that point on.

I wanted to interrupt ... 'HELLO ... did you *HEAR* what your colleague just shared?' Of course, I didn't intervene in their business (as tempting as it was) but mused over what I expected would eventually follow, which was this...

The report would probably continue to 'drop the ball' more frequently but for very different reasons to this example.

As his manager failed to recognize his struggles, he would feel demotivated and fed up that his appeal for some assistance had fallen on deaf ears.

Which would naturally lead to his resignation and a smug manager reaffirming to everyone he was correct in his opinion about his team member's poor performance, obviously taking no responsibility for his lack of empathy or poor management skills.

Had his manager acknowledged his struggle and discussed ways to support him, I imagine his team member would re-engage with more gusto and drive. And I wouldn't be sharing this story now!

Authenticity

People see through smoked mirrors. When our authenticity is absent, our communication comes across as stilted, off, and just wrong! So, in these situations, your teams will draw their own misguided conclusions.

A strong leader shows up in their own truth, warts, and all! And you know what? This is the glue that connects people. If you make a mistake. Own it. People will respect you for it and you will also be setting the gold standard for others to follow.

If you are a *Fresher* and new to the organisation, you might still be finding your feet. Perhaps at this early stage of your new journey, you don't know as much information as others or you might not have access to all the answers yet. Don't fret that you will be judged because this is probably only your perception and not reality.

It's totally ok not to be up to speed. Don't pretend you are or that you know it all. Eventually the truth will come to light, and this is what breeds mistrust and disengagement. They might wonder what else you might be lying about?

Authentic leadership is having the courage to show up as you.

Some of you may know Sara Blakely, founder, and inventor of the billion-dollar business Spanx. She is a hoot! During the first lockdown here in the UK, I found myself aimlessly scrolling through Instagram one day and stumbled across some of her posts. I was hooked. Why? They were comical, authentic, honest, and depicted her real 'upside down' family life on this social media platform.

Apart from the fact that she is a born entertainer and a hilarious raconteur, what is so enticing to watch is this. To many, she appears to have the perfect 'shiny' life and family. Yet she isn't afraid to share the many trials and tribulations she experiences just like the rest of us in our day-to-day drudgery.

In one of her many entertaining posts, she shared how she left the house, juggling four children under the age of seven, unintentionally wearing mismatched shoes! It was very funny! Did we respect her brilliant business acumen any less because of it? Absolutely not. In fact the opposite. We loved her more because of it. She is endearing and engaging. She doesn't alter her persona to fit her work-life, she is unapologetically herself both personally and professionally.

I'm not suggesting you intentionally turn up to the office wearing mismatched shoes but what I am saying is show up as the genuine, authentic, imperfect version of yourself because this is what draws and connects people to you.

Respect

No conversation should ever take place without mutual respect, irrespective of position or balance of power. It is one of the greatest catalysts of relationship breakdown in the workplace and once respect is lost, it is extremely hard to restore.

In more mediations than I care to remember, one of the most frequently discussed points related to respectful communication. We would often debate what that looked liked to each individual because for all of us that will be a different experience.

Participants might have been seeking acknowledgment when they had felt ignored, unheard or their opinions dismissed in meetings. Or they wanted their manager to stop crossing boundaries by contacting them outside of working hours.

Disrespect might be a blatantly aggressive and rude interaction or a more subtle behaviour like interrupting others midstream, over-talking, discarding ideas without giving them any airtime, laughing at a suggestion that was not intended to be funny. Then of course there are the non-verbal displays of disrespect. Eye rolling, frowning, smirking.

One mediation I facilitated was nearly derailed because of an incident of eye rolling!

In leadership, there is no place for disrespectful communication. Culture starts at the top and it's up to you to demonstrate the behaviour you want others to follow.

Transparency

At challenging times, your teams and colleagues don't want you to' fluff' around the issues. They deserve clarity, honesty, and transparency. They would prefer you to lay your cards on the table and say it how it is. While the news may not always be what they want to hear, they will respect you more for your candour rather than sugar coating it and hiding facts which will lead to greater mistrust.

A few years ago, I was talking to a client about a tricky situation she often found herself in.

Team members would often approach her, complaining about their colleagues but unwilling to give her permission to share their identity when she discussed the concerns.

In order to maintain confidentiality, she never revealed her source when she addressed the complaints and consequently was met with a barrage of animosity and backlash because of it.

And so, two things happened. Her teams went on a witch hunt seeking the identity of the complainant, ruffling feathers along the way. This sparked mistrust and disbelief because without concrete evidence, they questioned the veracity of the complaints.

A more effective approach might be to investigate why the complainant won't disclose their identity and what's sitting underneath that behaviour. I will explain more on this in Chapter 10.

Your role as a leader is be totally transparent in your management and communication because *tell, hide, and seek* behaviours do nothing more than incite frustration and mistrust. Is that a culture you wish to lead by?

Exploratory and Journaling Questions:

1. What can you do to build better relationships with your teams?

2. How well do you think you listen? On a scale of 1-10, what would you score?
3. Where could you use curiosity to improve the outcome of your difficult conversations?
4. Think of a leader, public figure, or someone you admire, which H.E.A.R.T quality do they demonstrate in their communication?
5. Which H.E.A.R.T. pillar is missing in your leadership style?

8

COMMUNICATION RULES

"People will forget what you said, people will forget what you did, but people will never forget how you made them feel".

— *MAYA ANGELOU*

It always makes me laugh when communication is referred to as those *nice to have* soft skills because I think they are the hardest to master. They are central to the success of all relationships and a harmonious workplace. Why then are the importance of communication skills overlooked, dismissed, or not honoured with the status they deserve?

It's Good to Talk

At the very start of my mediation career, I spent some time talking to HR Directors about people problems within their organisations. I wanted to get a handle on the type of issues that were inciting friction and roadblocks.

One day, a friend invited me into his company to speak with their Chief People Officer. When I arrived, I sensed what I can only describe as a *lightness* about the atmosphere. Everyone I was introduced to seemed carefree and well... happy!

I sat in their cafeteria and chatted for a couple of hours with the CPO. She had worked there about ten years and I commented on what I had observed.

I asked her why she thought that was. She smiled.

"We talk to each other!" She replied. "Problems don't get buried or brushed aside. They are dealt with. We have a culture of respect, openness and safety. No-one should ever feel inhibited to share a concern, regardless of their position. And our managers are trained and skilled to have those uncomfortable conversations so yes, we do have a happy workforce. And a happy workforce is a productive one!"

She made it sound so easy. And there it was. Utopia!

I wanted to bottle that up and often remembered it when I worked with businesses whose culture couldn't be more conflicting. The message was clear. It's good to talk!

Presence and Communication

Strong communication starts with presence. Have you ever been guilty of chatting with a team member or colleague and during the conversation, your phone pings or a notification pops up. You casually reach for it while allegedly still listening. But are you still giving them your undivided attention because now your focus is elsewhere?

To put this is some sort of context, I assume you wouldn't

pause a client presentation to cheekily scroll through your new Instagram reels. Of course you wouldn't because the risk of doing so would probably cost you the contract. Likewise there are risks to your other relationships too which also carry a high price tag if you behaved in this vein. The cost of tension and friction leading to time-consuming, stressful conflict. So focus on your audience and not your phone!

Different Modes of Communication

Years ago, the telephone was our primary communication tool... Yes I know, I'm showing my age! Nowadays, with the advent of new technology, there are numerous other instantaneous options available to us; email, Whatsapp, Voxer, Messenger.. and more! However all these new alternatives present their own set of problems.

Our reliance on written communications and messaging means the art of the conversation can be lost which gives rise to misunderstandings, triggered reactions, and message ping pong which ironically is also quite time consuming, time wasting, frustrating and stressful. We devote too much head space over-analysing the message, re-reading it, asking others their interpretation of it, crafting replies, mulling it over when we could be using our valuable time more effectively.

Each tool has an appropriate use but sometimes we fall into bad habits or opt for a lazy option which might not be the most suitable in the circumstances or draw the best outcome.

Do you evaluate whether a phone call or chat over a coffee would be more beneficial than a lengthy email to discuss changes to a document?

Or consider this situation if your team member is en-route to a client meeting and some key information comes to light that will impact the conversation. A phone call will be a much faster, safer and more reliable method than sending a message or email they might not see until after the meeting.

A delicate behavioural conversation might be more effective in person.

Or sometimes a brief call to explain a point might be a far better use of time and elicit an immediate answer instead of time-consuming exchanges of emails. Remember the example I shared in Chapter 5 with the manager and her assistant who couldn't locate mistakes in her work?

What about video meetings? These can raise all sorts of other complications.

When we are visible on camera, we sometimes forget we are being watched and scrutinised. I'm sure we've all seen our associates checking emails and taking calls during these conversations. Fidgeting, eyes darting everywhere except at the person speaking. Again, would we do this in a face-to-face meeting? No. So why do it here? Maybe it's draining and our attention span is reduced staring for long periods of time at a few square inches on our screens? Whatever the reason, it's a disrespectful communication. If you were meeting with a client, imagine the impression this would leave? Disinterest? Boredom?

Don't be concerned to share what behaviours and standards of professionalism you expect in conference video calls. In the event of extenuating circumstances where they need to take an urgent call or temporarily leave the meeting, ensure they understand what that looks like.

All this information could expressed be via email, a written clause in your handbook or a standard attachment with the meeting invitation.

Trust me, it's more comfortable to raise all this before an incident rather than afterwards.

I bet we've all experienced a 'Pyjama Gate' at one point over the last few years!

I'm referring to team members who are still donning their night wear at midday. Now I'm not judging! If you have a relaxed culture and that poses no problem *and* your teams are working productively, happy days!

If however you expect them to show up for meetings online, camera turned on and suitably attired, you need to share what that looks like and inform them that this is a company policy. The way we dress is a communication in itself. T-shirts and jeans might be the preferred style of one business yet shirt and tie might be expected by another. Every business globally will have a different expectation of what that looks like so ensure your teams are clear about it too.

As for camera shy participants, that conversation requires some cautious digging and exploration. Of course the cause may be an internet issue as *camera on* is sabotaging the quality of the call. However if it is a simply a case of choosing to hide behind the lens, this is a communication in itself.

It's time for them to understand *why* it's important and that falls on you to explain.

Again, it refers back to expectations of professional behaviours and standards and dare I say it values. If your teams or colleagues prefer not to show their face, are they the right fit for your culture?

Knowing Your Audience

We have explored different methods of communication, but I would like to move on now to those on the receiving end of it. Your audience.

I know many people who hate chatting on the phone, while others only correspond through email or text with messenger or Whatsapp and some who even chose to DM through Instagram. It's horses for courses.

Knowing your audience and their favoured method will ensure your communication is so much smoother.

While you may consider it an indulgence, adapting to their preference has its' benefits. If you are aware that a colleague or team member is overwhelmed by lengthy emails, they might skim through the content or fail to read it at all. If however you summarise it in brief bullet points, you will have more certainty they *do* read it and probably receive a much quicker response. I know that I often put long emails aside until I have the time to digest the content and sometimes that takes a few hours, if not days!

On the other hand, if the recipient is a detail person and your communication is too brief, this can be perceived as rude and can have negative consequences too. The key here is awareness, versatility, and elasticity.

But what about your communication with clients. Do you adapt your style and frequency of contact depending on their needs? Some would expect daily check-ins with you by phone. Others might prefer a weekly report or would only anticipate contact from you at monthly meetings. Be clear exactly what this looks like at the start of your relationship, because if they feel neglected or *unloved*, this might lose you the contract!

Communication is Two Way

When I worked in PR many moons ago, we would regularly attend brainstorms or focus groups to inspire creativity for client pitches We were all invited to share ideas, yet it wouldn't be uncommon for our MD to be met with a wall of silence. Except for those bold colleagues who were clearly in her *'inner circle'*.

She had no qualms about shutting us down or publicly humiliating us if a suggestion fell short of her expectations

Yet she, the Agency and ultimately our clients probably lost out on some truly innovative and top-notch brainwaves because of fear of ridicule.

Psychological safety did not feature as a priority in the Agency culture. Heaven forbid if we complained to HR or raised a Grievance. In those days, HR's role, certainly at our company, was to hire and fire.

We either put our head down or walked. Which was a shame because it was such fun!

So, time for some truth bombs!

Do you *inspire* or *inhibit* your teams to speak up?

Do you encourage and welcome all suggestions no matter how silly they may at first sound? Somewhere in the vast melting pot of concepts, designs and notions there might be a tiny seedling ready to be nurtured, developed and heralded as *the* next big idea!

But is there another layer to explore here? Perhaps it's not a fear that silences others but lack of opportunity.

Maybe with all the fire and excitement you bring with your energy, you offer no space for others to voice theirs. And that's when creativity is stifled and resentment brews.

So as a leader be mindful of sharing not just your thoughts

but also the floor to give others the same opportunity to allow for those important exchanges to flow freely.

If you continue to hit walls of silence, investigate what's behind that and if nothing substantial shows up, I would recommend some deep introspection to reflect on your own behaviours.

Psychological Safety – The Impact of Non-Verbal Communication

As a leader or business owner, you have a duty of care to provide both physical and psychological safety to your employees. What does that look like?

I wonder if you have stopped to think how you are being experienced? You might believe you are a *pussy cat*, a pushover, because you possess a big, caring heart and your intention is only one of kindness and support. However, your non-verbal communication is shouting otherwise. It's roaring scary *Lion*!

Let's use a performance conversation as an illustration of my point. In this scenario your team member might be drowning under pressure, and this has triggered a series of mistakes in her work.

She is feeling overwhelmed with the amount of tasks on her plate. So you arrange a check in with the intention of investigating what's going on. Yet when you meet face to face and ask her for examples, she shuts down, blankly repeating that she can't offer up any examples, which is frustrating for you. How can you support her if you don't understand what needs fixing?

So, you ask again with an affirmation that you want to understand and help. In your sweet calm, *pussy cat* voice (your perception) yet your body language, energy and intonation is screaming *impatience*.

This is when your words and non-verbal communication are out of alignment. It is little wonder she shuts down. She finds the whole experience nerve wracking and *you* overwhelming.

This is where positional perspective is useful.

You view this as an exasperating conundrum. If she could *just* get her words out, it would be easy to identify the problem and formulate a constructive plan to move forward.

She on the other hand is so nervous of you and worried about her job security, she believes this might be her last chance saloon (her narrative not fact). Her *Fight Flight or Freeze* response has kicked in and she has *frozen*.

Her limiting belief is ... this could be *sayonara!*

And this is all down to your non-verbal communication. Can you see the chaos it has generated?

What then is the panacea?

Check in with yourself and perform a quick communication self-audit. Are your words, energy, presence, and state in harmony? Or are they sending out conflicting messages? Notice your impatience and the language you use. Are they equally tempered?

Now consider a more useful state. What would that look like? Calmer, less frantic, present, softly spoken? More *pussy cat* and less *lion*?

Imagine yourself in the same conversation in your transitioned and gentler state, do you believe you would draw a more successful outcome? I think so.

Launder Your Language

There are some words that are and always will be triggering and they can easily put someone's back up. These are *'you'* accusations.

"*You* said blah blah"

"*You* did xyz"

The problem with *you* statements is that they can provoke denial.

"No, I didn't". "That's incorrect". "Not true."

They make the conversation personal rather than about *the behaviour*. Instead try "I observed that" or "I feel that" because these words position *your* perspective and *your* experience, and no-one can argue with that!

And then there are the *'Yes but-ters'*...

'Yes, but' is not helpful! This response signifies you've totally dismissed anything your conversational partner has said leading up to that moment. You have chosen not to hear, acknowledge, absorb, or consider their points and that can elicit more tension and reduce the opportunity for success.

Try instead *'Yes and'*. The difference here although small, gives you the opportunity to not only acknowledge their points but also to add yours.

Change ... *'Yes, but that idea is far too complicated'* To... *'Yes, that might work AND how about we brainstorm ways to simplify it'*.

In certain circumstances *should* is another inflammatory word. And here's one good reason why you *shouldn't* use it. Although advice may be well meaning, if it's uninvited, it's instantly discarded and thrown out with the bath water because none of us like to be *told* we are doing it wrong or how we *should* do it.

This is a familiar mistake many leaders or business owners make. They try to 'convince' others to invest in their grand plans or influence change yet they are missing a beat. Imposing your ideas, albeit very good ones (in your opinion), is not the most constructive way to encourage a shift in the decision-making process. In fact it will probably have the adverse effect.

The more we are told we *should* do something, the more entrenched we become and the more we dig our heels in and decide we shouldn't, without giving any thought or consideration to the merit of the idea.

As you now know, there are more subtle ways of influencing using curiosity of course!

A few examples ...

'Have you considered this option?'

'What do you think about this idea?'

'What are your views on this?'

Reframing confrontational language is a great tool to diffuse conflict whether it's your own challenging interaction or you are managing team disputes. This takes the sting out of the conversation, calms the hostility, and brings back a little decorum.

When a team member is seething with anger about their colleague's behaviour and claims:

"He was rude and aggressive."

Try this reframe:

"I can hear you don't appreciate his tone or the way he spoke to you."

Or another example:

"She's so disrespectful. She always interrupts and cuts me off mid-sentence."

To this reframe:

"You would like her to listen to you and allow you to finish before sharing her opinion."

What about the word *No!*

I'm sure not many of us like to hear it, but sometimes it's a necessity! These two letters can be antagonistic, inflammatory and breed contempt!

It can feel like a rejection. A closed door. A finite end.

You might need to offer up an unexpected *'no'* when a team member was expecting you to approve their 'in office' days.

Or it may be a *'no'* to a colleague because you disagree with their idea.

It might be a *'no'* to a client because they are expecting you to include additional work that falls beyond the perimeters of the agreed project.

It provokes staggering reactions. Disbelief. Shock. Tantrums. Raised voices.

"What do you mean you WON'T approve my days?"

"What's wrong with the idea?!"

"Why WON'T you take on the project?"

So how do you still say *'no'*, without actually using the word?

There is a workaround and it's similar to the *Yes / No* game we used to play as children. The point is to soften the response by avoiding the actual word yet still acknowledging their request.

For example, try any of the following:

To your teams:

"That could be tricky, can we look at other days instead of Tuesday that week?"

To your colleagues:

"Thank you for your input. Let's keep going and explore more options."

To your clients:

"I would be happy to quote for this or discuss it as a separate piece of work".

While I accept that it's not always possible to avoid the word, why not consider and practise other options that still convey your message but with less provocation!

Confusing Communication - Whose Fault Is It?

It's so easy to view other people as *the problem* if they don't understand or misinterpret what we say. I mean why wouldn't someone get our point? Although it might make total sense in our head and we believe we have explained it with great clarity, sometimes it's not as obvious as we imagine. We need to acknowledge that, own it and accept responsibility for it.

Often, we explain it again, in the same way two, three or four more times. And then we wonder why we are still met with confusion or vacant expressions.

As Albert Einstein said:

"Insanity is doing the same thing over and over and expecting different results."

We need to drop our ego and find a better way to communicate to our audience at a level and pace they will comprehend. And here's one method to help with that... *'What not If'*.

Have you noticed how your teams nod enthusiastically in meetings, indicating they have understood a task or instructions... but clearly haven't grasped a word? Yet this only comes to light too late when the task has been badly executed or in fact not executed at all.

This affirmation could be for many reasons. They are people pleasers and think if they show agreement, they will score brownie points. They are afraid to speak up for fear of ridicule by team members. Or it could be that they simply haven't understood!

Instead of asking *if* they have understood, try asking *what* they have understood.

This will help to:

- Highlight any obstacles that they need support to overcome.
- Give you all the opportunity to address any misunderstandings.
- Explain anything in greater detail that is still unclear.

An effective way to do this without sounding patronizing is to ask them to share their understanding of the conversation to ensure you are all on the same page.

By the way, this also works very well with partners and children!

Written Communication – Dos and Don'ts

Written communication presents an abundance of potential pitfalls as I have alluded to in previous chapters.

Here are a few pointers to minimise the risk of a reactive response and ensure optimum success for your communication.

- Don't overcomplicate your message. If you can write it in fewer words, do so. This doesn't mean that you

should cut the content down or skimp on pleasantries but keep it succinct and clear. Unless of course you are a lawyer and there is a requirement to use specific, complicated words and legal jargon!
- Names are important to people and we are protective of them. Ensure for example Danielle is not spelt as Daniella or Victoria isn't abbreviated to Vicky. Unless you have permission, or they have specifically expressed that is their preference. If you aren't sure, ask!
- Re-read your email or message back before sending it. I have been the subject of many embarrassing moments where autocorrect has made its' own assumptions for my intention. Although this is a very helpful tool, it can totally change the tone and meaning so take heed!
- Remember the recipient can't hear your intonation or read your expression. Take that into account to minimize misinterpretation. Use perspective before hitting *send*, if you were sitting in their shoes, how would you receive it and would it make total sense?
- If the email is long or complicated, pre-warn the recipient first that it's on its way. Use this as an opportunity to discuss anything you would like to highlight or bring to their attention.

Timely Communication - Don't Leave them Hanging

Let's talk about the waiting game.... when your team member is patiently expecting a response from you or when you have made a promise to report back and all they hear is crickets. Situations like...

- Confirmation of their pay review
- Authorization on their change of days in the office
- Approval from *your* manager about their promotion
- Verification of their role in a project
- Sign off on their holiday dates

While this may be placed at the bottom of your *urgent* pile, it may be of huge significance to them. Not responding in a timely manner will always have consequences, for them and your relationship. Assumptions will be drawn and the sting (that they are not valued) will resonate long after the event.

And this was cause of a great deal of pent-up resentment in a mediation between a manager and one of her teams, who I'll call Abigail.

While Abigail was anticipating with bated breath for her holiday dates to be authorised, her manager took three days to reply to her email.

Not only did she miss out on the gorgeous cottage by the sea she had been so excited to book, but she also felt extremely bitter towards her manager for sitting on her request so long. Her conclusion was she was not a respected or valued member of the team.

The truth was simply that her manager had been caught up in meetings and other pressing issues. However, had she taken five minutes out of her day to check those dates and hit reply, the horizon might have looked very different for both of them. A much better relationship, a week's holiday booked by the coast, no time-consuming mediation or endless hours ruminating over what might have been.

My advice:

- If you make a commitment, honour it, and specify the timeframe to manage your team member's expectations.
- Form new habits and create systems to ensure these requests don't' slip through the net.
- Take heed from this story that responses should be placed higher up the urgent pile!

Courageous Communication

One of the most inspirational people I follow is Brené Brown. In fact, she was the primary reason I pursued this journey. Her work and teachings have helped me overcome many obstacles and *get out of my own way* on numerous occasions! If you haven't read any of her books, watched her Ted Talks or viewed her Netflix talk, I recommend you do.

Brown is known for her work on vulnerability and courage. I have explained the importance of authentic communication in Chapter 7 and now I would like to explain how courage is connected to it.

Leadership courage is putting yourself *out there*, despite how scary that might feel. It is laying your cards on the table and confessing that:

- 'You don't have the answer'

- 'You've made a mistake'
- 'You don't understand'
- 'You're not certain'

'But you're damn well going to make this right or source the answer and you will come back to them on this'.

And then do that! And if for any reason this isn't possible, convey that. Keep others in the loop.

Honesty goes hand in hand with courage. If you make that commitment, follow through. Honour it. People will respect you for it rather than judge you because of your lack of it.

These are conversations that breed trust and build bridges.

Remember …. Honesty, Courage and Authenticity are a pipeline for connection rather than a barrier to communication!

Clarity and Cross Functional Communication

I have spoken with many stressed out employees over the years who reported into several managers across different departments. It came as no surprise they were angry and bitterly resentful towards their bosses for not backing them when the proverbial *s**t hit the fan.*

Their intention was to always perform their best for each one individually but splitting themselves three ways was taxing, confusing and hectic. Each manager expected *their* workload to take priority without considering the impact on their team member or quality of work. The employees felt like were caught between the devil and the deep blue sea.

Their emotional health would suffer when they stayed late night after night to keep up. They became exasperated and disengaged because their managers were both disinterested in their excuses for the tardy completion of an assignment and unaccepting that other managers' work took precedence over theirs. This attitude made them the *conflict filling* of a manager sandwich which was unfair.

During these awkward and demanding times, your employee may not have the courage, will or confidence to have that straight talking conversation with you or the other managers.

And I get it. It's not easy. Particularly if everyone is precious and uppity about the importance of their own work.

Here's the solution to keep all your relationships sweet.

When you allocate an urgent piece of work to your team member, check what else they have on their plate which is equally pressing. Their reaction will be quite revealing. I'm guessing you will see one of two responses. Panic and protestations that they are overloaded or silence as they shut down worrying how on earth to juggle so many balls.

However, you won't know this for sure, unless you ask.... Here's a good use of curiosity!

It's your responsibility to collaborate with the other managers in an adult and professional manner. Not ignore the problem and expect your report to sink under the pressure.

And then convey back what has been agreed to your team member, while also encouraging them to speak up and voice their concerns with all of you before the situation builds up to a full-blown crisis. This of course would require a culture of psychological safety... but I think you probably know that by now!

Your employee will recognize and appreciate that you have their back and feel relieved that the pressure has been alleviated. You will all have clarity and understanding about expectations and deadlines. It's a win / win!

And if you are met with resistance and opposition from your fellow colleagues, Chapter 10 will support you through those tricky interactions!

What's Your Communication Style?

It wouldn't be right to end this chapter without some reflection on your communication style. It's probably clear by now from the chapter on communication how toxic and damaging the wrong approach can be.

How would your style fare?

Do you define it as ambiguous, confusing, chaotic, brash or overpowering?

Or would you consider yourself an over-giver, under giver, or a *broadcaster*?

Let me leave you with this introspective practice and reflective ending to the chapter!

Exploratory and Journaling Questions:

1. What is your preferred method of communicating? Do you believe it is always the most appropriate?
2. How well do you consider your audience in all your communications?
3. Do you believe you have crafted a culture of psychological safety?
4. What does a courageous conversation look like to you?
5. What steps will you take to improve your communication style?

9
FEEDBACK AND RECOGNITION

"Feedback is the Breakfast of Champions."

— *KEN BLANCHARD*

Woe betide those who dismiss the importance of feedback. Delivered well, it can open doors and strengthen team building and relationships. Conducted badly and it can shut down conversations and opportunities in minutes. I therefore think it's significant enough to warrant its own chapter!

What is the Purpose of Feedback?

The error so many *Freshers*, managers or business owners make is their misguided perception that feedback is a critique. They pounce on a mistake, besetting their teams with negativity, showering them with an assault of criticism, grinding their employee down until they are so demotivated, they disengage or throw the towel in.

This is not the purpose of feedback. Rather its role is to support their teams to move the needle towards their goals, to motivate and inspire them on their journey, to nurture and broaden their skills and to bring out the best of their abilities. To help showcase their strengths and develop their weaknesses.

So, let's explore feedback in more detail to ensure your conversations are more successful and the longer-term relationship is fortified.

Frequency and Consistency

So how frequently do you give feedback? As and when required? In weekly meetings or during formal appraisals?

There is little purpose raising an issue that took place 6 months prior in a bi-annual performance review. Your team member will probably have a hazy recollection of the event which means exploration of it will be pointless and difficult to discuss. Details will be foggy. It would come as no surprise if you encountered a defensive response without clarity of facts to justify your observations.

If you are tracking their performance and regularly and consistently checking in, you will avoid the shock and accusations that they have been blindsided as they didn't see *that* feedback coming.

Transparency and Honesty

This is a tough one for all the *People Pleasers* out there however as I have explained, it can get you into a whole lot of hot water if you don't acknowledge the importance of it or dedicate the time to it.

One of the most toxic mediations I have facilitated stemmed from a lack of transparency in feedback during a performance review.

The organisation was going through a reshuffle and in the interim their Head of Department stepped in to manage an experienced and long serving team member while they searched for a new line manager.

Faced with plenty more pressing concerns, her management approach to performance reviews was a touch too lax and laid back, leaving the employee proud as punch and confident that she was on track. Apart from a few minor tweaks, her report's understanding was she was doing ok.

The major concerns, of which there were several, were too challenging and timely to address. So her boss adopted a *laissez-faire* approach.

While they weren't impacting the employees' productivity and output, they were behavioural issues that were whipping up a storm in her relationships with colleagues, clients, and peers. For example, how she challenged and appeared to confront others in meetings if she disagreed, which was not appreciated.

The Head of Department's viewpoint was *manage the manageable* and the fractured relationships would take a back seat for the time being.

But that's not a realistic assessment and I'm sure you can imagine what followed when the new line manager was appointed.

All hell let loose. It was carnage.

Her initial reaction to her team member was disbelief that she spoke to colleagues in that manner and more interestingly that this hadn't been raised as a concern before. She was faced with not one but two challenges.

How to delicately address the behaviour in this fresh relationship and weighing up whether she was too new *in post* to question why her own boss had essentially *advocated* the disrespectful conduct by ignoring it. She was caught between a rock and a hard place.

No doubt the new line manager danced cautiously around the problematic behaviour because of their *immature* and tenuous relationship. With little time devoted to building rapport and connection because of her recent arrival, I imagine this only served to intensify the angst between them and this story reconfirms again the value of good relationship in successful feedback.

Every attempt to tackle the issue was met with hostility and accusations of bullying from her team member. After all, the Department Head had no problem with her report's communication, so why did she?!

Eventually a grievance was raised by the employee against her line manager which was drawn out for months and months. The team member was signed off for stress related sick leave, the manager's own emotional health suffered immeasurably as she questioned her own capabilities and the worrying lack of support from the organisation.

As for the Head of Department, I still wonder what learnings, if any, she drew from this whole sorry mess. However I do know that honest and transparent feedback at the start would have been pivotal in transforming the path ahead for all of them.

So, what held her back? Absence of skills? Fear? A shortage of time?

If this resonates, I suggest you identify why and then refer to

Chapters 6 and 7 for guidance managing these daunting conversations more confidently and efficiently.

Just as a side note here, if time is your justification for your abstinence, consider how much more of it you will be forced to dedicate to lengthy investigations if you take this preferred route!

How Do You Present It?

There is a great deal of debate around the best delivery method of feedback. Are you a believer in the *'feedback sandwich'* or do you prefer a more direct approach? As we all know, the way it is delivered dictates how it is received, absorbed, processed and the different responses it can provoke.

So, this is my take on it…

'Drip' Feed

This is a frustrating method as your teams don't get the full picture in one hit. They expend too much time and energy trying to work it out without sufficient direction from you (as illustrated in the example in Chapter 5). Or they waste too much time filling in the gaps and joining the dots only to find critical pieces of the puzzle are missing and they are stuck, unable to push forward on a project or task without additional information.

'Spoon' Feed

Your role as their leader is to nurture and support your teams to develop and grow and part of this process is self-awareness and reflection. If you give them *all* the information, it leaves no opportunity to work anything out for themselves or think for themselves limiting their learning potential if everything is handed to them on a plate?

'Force' Feed

Is your style to bombard your teams with feedback so they feel totally overwhelmed and overloaded with information? This makes it near impossible to process and gives rise to panic and confusion, leaving them unsure where to even start, caught in a depth of a big, dark abyss!

Making Time

Feedback shouldn't be rushed. Schedule it at a convenient time for both of you and avoid sandwiching it between meetings or deadlines taking your attention and presence away from the conversation.

Be mindful too of what is going on at the time for your team member. I don't mean just within the workplace. While I don't expect you to be aware of the intricacies of their personal life, if you are conscious the conversation might stimulate a response, bear in mind the impact this will have in the grander scheme of things when you diarise it.

I'm not suggesting you put it off altogether, however I do suggest that you acknowledge and empathise with any hardships they are experiencing at the start of your conversation to avoid a combustion of emotion as your feedback might be the straw that broke the camel's back.

I have witnessed this all too often. When an employee is trying hard to hold it all together and then that one piece of negative feedback tips them over the edge.

Be Curious

Feedback conversations are the perfect opportunity to use curiosity. Not just to explore *why* things are going off track but also as a benchmark to measure your team member's thoughts about their performance before you jump in. As I alluded to above, if you're managing your teams effectively, they should never feel blindsided by the information however a quick check in is always useful.

This will be valuable data to gauge how to begin and which direction to drive the conversation. Think of it as a guiding compass. For example, their perception of where they are and what the problems are, might be way off track to your observations.

Let's take this scenario.

You may have received several complaints from colleagues or clients about your team member's behaviour in a meeting citing them as a tad confrontational, arrogant, and rude.

So, you ask your employee how they thought that particular meeting went earlier in the week, waiting of course for any indication of bad feeling or an altercation. This is assuming of course they possess some self-awareness or confidence to share an honest account of what happened.

If their perception was that it went well, then the news you are about to deliver may come as a complete surprise.

So where do you start?

Share your feedback and ask them what they think about these complaints.

You may be hit with one of two responses:

Option 1…Your ideal response!

"Oh! I had no idea. I'm concerned to hear that. Could you possibly give me some examples?"

This demonstrates self-reflection and a willingness to understand and change their behaviour. The conversation will probably be a much smoother one from here onwards.

Option 2 ... A more common and confrontational reaction.

"I would like to know **who** *exactly* made these allegations?"

They will no doubt embark on a *witch hunt* seeking the source of the accusations, shutting down and refusing to accept responsibility for their behaviour. Now you have a clear indication how to proceed with this review because this situation requires a little more tact and caution!

So why are they defensive and triggered?

They feel under threat or *under attack*! Their *Fight, Flight or Freeze* response is activated and jumping into action again. Continue using curiosity in a similar vein. Use *the traffic light* system. Manage their state before attempting to manage the behaviour.

"Tell me what happened in the meeting."

Listen back for their response. Offer no judgement at this point. This is an information gathering exercise. An opportunity for them to be heard and for you to demonstrate empathy which we all know quietens rage and indignation.

"Why do you think they might have shared this feedback with me?"

Continue until you sense they are in a calm enough state to move the conversation forward and address the real reason you're there!

If the feedback conversation is with a colleague or client, curiosity is a good tool to explore their understanding of how you arrived at the situation you now find yourself in and will help your positioning of your perspective too.

The Power of Positive Feedback - It's not all bad!

Feedback can of course be positive too! It can come in several guises. Verbal acknowledgement and recognition as well as appreciation by way of a gift or an award. And if you doubt the impact of this, reflect on how you felt when you have been recognized with a prize or honour in your lifetime. I'm certain it inspired you to do even greater things!

It is an affirmation of a job well done, a thank you from a customer or an observation from a colleague. It increases engagement and retention and is the fodder that drives, motivates, and pushes the needle in their endeavours, demonstrating to your teams they are valued and held in high regard.

Remember also to acknowledge those people who have excelled for making extraordinary effort which for others has been *effortless*.

Be mindful of course that we all like to be recognized in different ways. This is where the value of relationships is key to understand what makes others tick and who they are.

Don't assume that your team member would prefer a public display of praise in a weekly team meeting (particularly if they are shy or an introvert). A private audience with you without all the fanfare is possibly a more comfortable way for them to receive it.

And what about if you chose to *gift* a thank you instead of verbal feedback for recognition of excellence or effort. I recommend you tailor these accordingly because a proper thank you is personal and subjective to the person receiving it.

If you know one team member is saving money towards their 'new home' fund, a financial reward would be appreciated far more than Amazon vouchers. If you have another employee who loves knitting jumpers as a hobby, I have no doubt she would be blown away by a bag of beautifully coloured balls of wool.

So How Do You Like Yours?

We all like to receive it in different ways. Some like it delivered without *faff*, straight and to the point. Others prefer it cushioned and positioned more gently. However one way that often grates is uninvited feedback, particularly from someone who you have little rapport with.

I never really reflected on this until an incident a few years ago. And this certainly gave me some insight into how it feels to be on the receiving end of badly executed and unwanted feedback. It has opened my eyes to the realisation that delivered thoughtlessly provokes, triggers, and repels while done well, can feel supportive and be appreciated and open door to new possibilities.

Now of course I'm sure we have all had a dose of unkind and harsh feedback throughout our lives. In our formative years at school we may have experienced our teacher's red ink scribbles across our homework or nasty jibes in the playground.

During our teens and into adulthood, we may have received a backlash of verbal feedback from friends about our fashion style or the way we play sport. We might have been the recipient of unsolicited feedback on social media such as LinkedIn sales messages advising us what *they* believe we need. Haven't we all at some point been the victim of cruel comments and criticism on Facebook and Instagram that can knock the stuffing and confidence out of us!

So, this was the experience that brought it to the fore to me a few years ago.

I had been working with a tech expert to address an issue on my website which she resolved quickly and efficiently. I sent her a thank you email and this was her response....

A critique of my website design that I had spent months creating (and loved) and a suggestion that it looked outdated, followed by a sales pitch outlining what improvements she could make.

To be honest, she had a couple of valid points but here is MY point. I hadn't asked for feedback so when she threw it in my face without checking if I was interested in hearing it or asking permission to share her opinion, yes ... I was triggered!

Now if she'd been wise, she would have nurtured a relationship with me and gauged how I felt about my website (knowing I designed it myself). She would have invested a little time to understand a bit about me and how I tick and then and only then, ask if I would welcome some constructive advice.

And that's one of the key takeaways with feedback, it's all about the relationship you have with the person giving it and how it's delivered.

Unless it is invited or part of a performance review, never assume people want it just because *you* think it will be useful!

The Impact and Importance of Recognition

Over the years I've learnt many valuable lessons from my work, but little more valuable than the importance of recognition.

Recognising achievements, struggles, effort, contribution.

Why have I included it in this chapter? I believe it goes hand in hand with feedback (delivered well). Both can draw the best from people and shine a light on them.

It encourages your teams to push through barriers that feel unmovable. To continue in the face of adversity. To spur them on to *'bring their A game'* and best endeavours to every situation. It is a vehicle to demonstrate to your teams they are valued, worthy and important.

In Zulu, there is a welcome greeting that encapsulates this beautifully...

"Sawubona"... which translates as "I see you; I notice you".

In every workplace you will find a variety of characters and personalities. Some will be attention seeking, loud and vociferous. And others, quieter and more subdued, industriously beavering away but without all the fanfare.

This is a perfect example of where *Sawubona* is impactful and a reminder to let these less raucous types know they are doing a sterling job because it is easy to shower the vocal and more noticeable team members with praise, a quick *high five* here and *well done* there and overlook their silent colleagues.

So perhaps you could employ this new greeting at the start of your next team meeting, your 1:1's or performance reviews! If nothing else your team will be very impressed by your linguistic skills!

If you have ever dismissed the impact of praise and recognition, I would like to share an experiment I heard about several years ago. It is a little bit *out there* and has been met with mixed opinions regarding the veracity of the results. I appreciate you may be a sceptic; however, I am *choosing* to accept it as an interesting learning.

Known as *The Rice Experiment*, it was conducted by Dr

Masaru Emoto to illustrate the negative and positive impact of our words on our emotions and behaviours which in feedback can be so impactful. He placed equal amounts of rice into three identical glass beakers pouring equal amount of water into each.

He labelled each beaker. One with *'Thank you'*, the next *'You're an idiot'* and the third *'Ignore'*. Every day for a month he spoke to the beakers according to the allocated label.

At the end of the thirty days, the first beaker that had been showered with gratitude and praise appeared to have fermented nicely and was a pleasant pearly white colour. The second beaker that had been belittled and *put down* had turned dark green and mouldy while the last one that had been disregarded was a disgusting shade of black.

If you are a believer, this will be a strong reminder of the power of positivity and praise to encourage and inspire your teams. It is similarly a cautionary warning of the adverse impression your negative and harsh words can leave as well of course of the biting impact of exclusion!

I have my own personal experience of this early on in my PR career. We had been working on the launch of a new pager for a client in the Telecom's sector. At the time, nearly thirty years ago, this was a big deal! We were attempting a simultaneous, nationwide, pager message to launch sites across the country announcing they had *gone live*. It was very complicated and as you can imagine there was ample opportunity for it to crash and burn on the day so attention to detail and preparation was crucial.

Although at that time I was only a junior executive, I was an integral member of the launch team of five. Six months of industrious work paid off and the launch was a huge success, receiving excellent press coverage and acclaim.

The client was over the moon, as were we! The following day every member of the team received a personal thank you from the MD sharing fantastic feedback. Except for me. I was gutted. I'm an *all or nothing* person and had dedicated every ounce of energy and love into this project which made it an even more bitter pill to swallow. I was deflated, demotivated and hurt. Although he realised his oversight and rectified it a few days later, the initial smart I felt stung for a long time afterwards. The fact that I still talk about it all these years later must indicate the impact it had on me at the time! My passion for the product and the client diminished after that event, as did my engagement, all because a 'thank you for a doing a great job' was forgotten.

I hope this explains how destructive the omission of positive feedback and recognition can be on morale and productivity and of course relationships within the business and as in this case, with clients too.

Why Does Feedback Fall Flat?

Let's look now at a few ways to improve the outcome of the feedback.

In the beginning:

We know the approach dictates the outcome so be mindful how you initiate the conversation. Think about your tone, your language, and your style. Be wary of confrontational accusations and *you* statements.

In person:

It's always my preference to have the conversation in person if possible. I believe it is easier to gauge how the feedback is being received and pick up on non-verbal signals that might be harder to spot online. Frustration, upset, confusion, anger. This gives you the opportunity to explore these emotions in the moment to ensure any problems are managed during the conversation and not left to fester.

Use curiosity:

Ask open ended questions as much as possible. Enquire how your team member thinks they're doing or how they think they might improve on a piece of work. Check if there's anything preventing them from achieving that. Explore obstacles and solutions together and iron out any possible blockades to future success.

Listen:

Use this superpower to ensure they feel heard too. They may consider your feedback is unjustified or unfair. Give them a voice and allow them to share their view and discuss it. Remember listening is respectful and doesn't mean you necessarily agree. As you know by now, it diffuses tension rather than escalates it.

Timing:

Raise your concerns or observations as soon as possible but consider the best time for it. Ideally when neither of you are stressed or overtired. It's never a good idea to embark on a challenging conversation at the end of a long day when energy is flagging. Unless you are offering praise and positive feedback to inspire, boost morale and confidence.

Don't overload:

If you have more than one concern to raise, prioritise one or two rather than bombarding them with several. They will not only be overwhelmed but shut down or pushback as their faithful *Fight, Flight or Freeze* response kicks in. Manage these first and once progress or improvements are visible, they will be better placed to take more feedback on board.

Consistency:

This is important if your team member reports to other managers particularly if the same specific concerns are coming up for all of you. Otherwise it may seem that you are picking on them and coming across more finicky and pedantic than your colleagues.

Share the impact:

Every action creates a reaction. Explain the effect of their action or behaviour. Communicate *why* it is particularly problematic. For example their infrequent communication might be frustrating a client who feels they are being neglected. Or their slow progress on a report might be generating delays to other departments and ultimately costing the business for missing a deadline.

Clarity:

Use specific examples to illustrate your points. Be direct and don't prevaricate. Remember the example in chapter 3 of the business owner whose subtle approach left his team member confused about the purpose of the conversation but well informed about the rules of tennis!

Review:

Mutually agree a realistic timeframe to assess progress. Arrange a follow up meeting so they are clear about expectations.

Recognition:

Monitor progress and remember to acknowledge and praise when you notice improvements.

Support:

Let them know you are there if they hit a bump. It's a team effort. They need to step up and make the change but ensure you are there for support if they encounter any obstacles.

Remember your M.A.P:

Manage your mindset. Be clear about the outcome and objectives of the conversation. Is your intention to nurture change, raise awareness of behaviours, motivate or boost morale and output? Prepare well.

I will discuss the best way to manage feedback with clients and your own boss in the next chapter, but I hope you have found some golden nuggets in this one to support you through these difficult managerial conversations which can very easily derail you or demotivate your teams.

Exploratory and Journaling Questions:

1. What's your feedback style?
2. Reflect on a time when you won an award or were recognized for an achievement. Note how you felt and the impact it made.
3. Do you offer praise and recognize achievements as much as negative feedback?
4. Where do you think your feedback falls short of success?
5. What action will you take to manage your feedback more effectively?

10

MANAGING THE CONVERSATIONS

"Be Brave Enough To Start A Conversation That Matters."

— *MARGARET WHEATLEY*

Now that you have been furnished with an abundance of tools, strategies, and guidance, let's take a more in depth look at how you can effectively and practically apply what you learnt in specific situations and conversations.

Managing Attitude, Apathy and Resistance

How do you manage attitude, apathy, and resistance?

Let's look for example at the response of *ok* when you ask a team member to do a job. *Ok* is a problematic communication because it is ambiguous. Does this reply indicate their understanding or is it tinged with a touch of attitude?

Do they mean:

"*Ok* yes I agree"

"*Ok* I'll do it"

Or are they indulging you with an *ok* simply to shut you up?

And this is where you'll need to use all your intuition and observational skills.

It is of course contextual and situational. An *ok* in response to 'can you just do xyz please' is a perfectly acceptable reply.

However, if it's an *ok* in response to a performance issue you've spent thirty minutes discussing, in my opinion that demonstrates a reluctant, slightly belligerent, and disrespectful attitude.

And my choice action here would be to dig a little deeper and investigate what's really going on behind the behaviour. Remember behaviours are a window into our world. You just need to look through the window and find the message.

If they don't appear to have absorbed the information, I would ask them to summarise *what* they have understood, not *if* they have understood. That way you both have clarity now how to move the conversation forward, correcting them if they've *misunderstood* and confirming if they *have understood*.

Let's take another example when you get hit with pushback and a response of "I don't want to do that" from one of your teams. This scenario was raised in a leadership training session.

The Department Head was taking some planned time out the business which meant her manager was required to step up and deputise in her absence.

For her to do this efficiently, my client felt her manager would benefit from some people management training to support her in this part of her role.

However, resistance kept showing up during the conversation as the manager was firmly against the idea.

So, what do you do when resistance is in the room? Explore why!

Was the resistance to the training or to managing people I wondered? Did the manager feel she was adequately experienced in this area so offended by the offer? Well in this case and after some discussion... it appeared not!

The manager simply didn't enjoy that part of her role, even though it was a fundamental part of her job.

So, this was what I suggested she do?

Check *why* she was resistant to levelling up and address *that reason* rather than *telling* her the training was obligatory.

Your teams can't dictate the terms of their role to suit them but equally it's important to know what was driving their defiance.

In this case, it became evident the manager loved and excelled in every other aspect of her job, yet simply didn't care to manage people.

So, I suggested she approached the conversation from a different angle to illustrate the importance of it, by asking her the following questions.

- What would happen if there was an emergency when my client (her boss) was on leave that she was ill equipped to deal with?
- Without the appropriate training, how would she manage it and what would the consequences be?
- What too would the impact be on her, the rest of the team and more importantly the wider impact to the rest of the business?

This made it real. This made it relatable. This made it something more than just *'managing people'*.

Instead of managing the behaviour, explore the resistance, manage what's at the core, explain *the why* and the bigger picture.

A word about apathy and assumptions.

Let's take the following example. How do you expect your team members to show up on their first day back at work after a week's holiday? Energised, refreshed, enthusiastic and motivated?

This might be how you return but it's not necessarily the same for everyone and here's where some perspective and objectivity are useful.

Last summer I returned home from a glorious week away in Greece feeling very *blah*!

Although I felt refreshed, I had no appetite or energy for work. My mojo was still bopping around in the blue Aegean Sea! Despite all the mindset tricks I practise, I still found myself stuck in *Lalaland* not quite ready to embrace the busy week ahead. Which is fine because I'm very lucky that I'm my own boss and I don't have to answer to anyone! But it made me question why I was feeling like this and what was behind this apathy. And once I unpicked it, I realised why it was affecting my mood and my behaviour.

So, what is the relevance of this story?

Sometimes your teams will come back from holiday feeling just like I did. Instead of expecting them to jump back in, refreshed and keen, check in with them. Not just a quick 'how was your holiday' but a genuine. 'How are you?'

I've worked with leaders who have been exasperated when a

team member returns from holiday demotivated and flat which creates resentment and friction with the rest of the team.

It's a common mistake to believe that just because they've had a break doesn't mean everything is hunky dory!

Explore why, remind them of their goals and drivers and discuss what support you can offer to avoid a longer-term holiday with no return date!

Managing Behaviours

Often, we take behaviours at face value meaning we deal with what is in front of our eyes. Sometimes they require further investigation to uncover what drives them and sits underneath them.

Behaviours are a gift. They are a window into our world and an expression of how we feel about a situation. They show our world view and what is important to us. Every behaviour is a message and demonstrates what we are feeling. The problem is that many people address the symptom (the behaviour) and not the cause of it.

Anger is often a response to frustration. Sarcasm is a reaction to hurt or fear.

In a video call for example, we see our colleagues and team members, checking emails, searching on google, scrolling through social media, distracted by their phones. This is a clear display of boredom. So, you might have words, berating them for their lack of participation, yet what you should be investigating is *why* they aren't they engaging?

Years ago, I facilitated a mediation between two senior executives who reported into the board. They were assigned to collaborate on a new, exciting venture together, but the relationship hit one too many bumps until it became untenable for them to work together.

One had an annoying habit of turning up late to meetings and taking control of them even though they weren't his to chair. He pointedly cc'd others into communications undermining his colleague and instructing her team which was not his responsibility. He crossed over the line.

During the mediation we discussed why he felt the need to act in this way which was evidently inciting frustration. After an hour or so of discussion, it became clear that his behaviours stemmed from his insecurities. He worried that people wouldn't take him seriously unless he *appeared to take control* and that was what he was attempting to do. Understanding this, we explored other ways he could show he was in control without stamping on his colleagues toes or winding others up.

Once we looked through *his* window, it became evident that his behaviour was a symptom of his fear.

Be aware of less obvious behaviours. Silence for example is a message demonstrating a fear or reluctance to speak up, why? Listen too for what isn't being said amongst the noise. That's another message that will be equally insightful but might require a little intuition and observation around non-verbal communication.

If an employee has been continuously missing deadlines or clocking in late, for example, your impulse might be to reprimand them and give them a warning. But here is where curiosity is the most helpful approach to explore what's behind the behaviour.

It could be the work is tardy because they are stuck and afraid to ask for guidance. Or it's possible they have been distracted by problems at home, worried about elderly sick parents or they have been suffering from sleep deprivation managing the joys of a teething baby. The outcome? They've been dropping the ball.

If you doled out a warning rather than investigating the behaviour, what do imagine would happen? I think it would increase their stress, add to their worry, and impact their performance further, possibly resulting in sick related absence.

Alternatively, having understood the reasons, you would I'm certain be more compassionate in your management of the situation by showing empathy, extending deadlines, offering all manner of support and perhaps taking some work away from them for the time being.

What about managing *disruptive* behaviours. I have heard many tales where some troublesome team members have spoilt team group training or masterminds and simply got away with it because the leader or trainer had no idea how to address their disrespectful actions.

In these circumstances, it is important to manage the behaviour as soon as possible. This is what I would suggest.

- Call a break at an opportune time during a training session. Quietly take the team member aside and have the conversations in private. It's imperative this is addressed swiftly and to communicate that the behaviour is unacceptable and will not be tolerated.
- Share what you observed and the impact it had on the group, the dynamics, and any individuals. Use curiosity. Ask their thoughts about your comments and explore what's driving their behaviour.
- Be clear about your objective. Do you want an apology and if so, who to? Are you expecting them

to withdraw from the training or just to discontinue the behaviour? Give them a voice and right to reply.
- Ensure they are crystal clear what next steps will be if the behaviour continues.
- If the behaviour has impacted other participants, don't brush it under the carpet or ignore the *elephant in the room*. It's important to acknowledge it and talk it through, giving them the opportunity to air their thoughts and feelings.
- If you are leading the day's activities, remember *your rules rule!* They are not open for negotiation but do ensure they are explained to all at the start of the day to manage expectations.

Managing Boundaries

How do you navigate these relationships when you are too close, too kind, or too accommodating to your team members? Situations when they take advantage of your good nature.

There will be instances when you need to say *no*. You might be forced to turn down their holiday request or have no option but to change the roster they asked for. They might be blown away! Shocked! They take it personally and this is when lovely relationships can turn sour.

Prevention is better than cure!

You need to set clear boundaries from the start so that *no* never feels personal. Identify what that looks like to both you and your teams otherwise assumptions will be made and that's when problems will seep through the woodwork.

Be mindful when they join the business how you view the

new relationship, your expectations of it and your own behaviours and actions which can be misleading.

The mistake many *Freshers* or new business owners make is that they want to ingratiate themselves with their teams. They might encourage an after-work drink or stepping out for a morning coffee. This is fine. But this is where the line should be drawn. Being super bubbly and *oversharing* too much personal information gives your employees the impression you are friends. And if they believe you are friends, their expectation is that the relationship is something it's not. And that's when you need to be cautious.

Boundaries work two ways. What lines do *you* cross with your teams? For example, do you require them to answer emails out of office hours. If so, has that been explained and do they understand and accept that? Do you contact them at weekends or during their holidays and expect them to respond just because that's what you would do?

What about those tricky situations where you are promoted over a colleague who is your good friend. Steering this new relationship from mate to manager can be precarious however there is a healthy way to be their boss and still maintain the relationship.

There may be unsaid expectations of loyalty or support (both ways) that will stir up hostility if this is challenged. It's important to address *the elephant in the room* and the intricacies of this new dynamic as early as possible. To add to the dilemma, be wary of hidden resentment if your colleague applied for the same promotion. This needs to be acknowledged.

How do you initiate that conversation?

- Invite them for a coffee but be honest and clear what the conversation is about. Don't blindside them or they will never trust you. The H.E.A.R.T framework would be very useful in this situation.
- Take the conversation outside the office.
- Discuss expectations from both perspectives and what that looks like for both of you. Acknowledge the relationship might change but reiterate you are still friends and hope that you will always enjoy an honest and open friendship.
- Discuss how you would both like to address possible issues as and when they crop up. Because trust me, they will! Make sure it is collaborative, so you have a reference point for the future that you are both committed to.
- Ask how your friend feels about your promotion? Resentful, jealous, angry? If they are anything but happy and proud for you, be mindful of that and discuss it. Don't leave it hanging or allow it to fester. This will only create problems down the line.
- It's starting to affect your relationship … now what? Acknowledge it and explore the reason, assuming they are open to talk it through. You could say that you are sensing some hostility / a bad feeling / some discomfort between you. Be authentic and honest in the hope that your friend will be too.

Managing Change and Transition

As I explained in Chapter 2, new processes and systems can be very unsettling and can certainly kick up some resistance.

However if you want to be an architect of change, you need to acknowledge that this takes some patience and perseverance.

- Explain the *why* behind the change.
- Highlight the benefits to them and the business and the positive impact it will ultimately make. Position it as an opportunity to support them, lighten their workload and make their job easier.
- Invite curiosity. Ask their opinion and encourage their contributions. If they feel included in the process, they will be more committed to it.
- If they still appear resistant, I would imagine something else is going on that requires some exploration. Use a coaching approach, keep digging until you reach the core of the issue. Are they afraid? If so, of what? Does the new technology frighten them? Why is this feeling so difficult. What's really going on for them?
- Listen to their concerns, acknowledge them and discuss what you can offer that will ease them into the new process. For example perhaps they can buddy up with a colleague to support each other through the transitional period. Or they might benefit from a 1:1 session with a colleague from your tech department.

Change isn't easy but if they have a positive mindset and believe that they can do it, they will!

Managing Client Conversations:

If you are an entrepreneur or consultant, these conversations can be very worrying. After all, there is potentially so much at stake.

There are a plethora of situations that might crop up but let's look at a few examples.

Imagine if you have dropped the ball or you haven't been in contact with your client as often as you should. You know you are in line for a justified *dressing down* and this amplifies your stress levels as you anticipate the conversation. Planning is therefore key to prepare yourself and your responses for the best outcome and to reduce your anxiety. While you may still endure the wrath of your client's harsh words, you will probably manage the dialogue more successfully than you anticipated.

A contentious question I'm often asked is how to chase invoices without appearing pushy, losing your rag, or losing the contract. How you manage it does depend on several factors. How late the payment is. Whether you have chased it before. Your relationship with your client and whether it is an ongoing issue or you are seeking payment for a one-off project.

Assuming you have sent a few gentle reminders which have been ignored, I would suggest trying the following:

- Speak to the client directly, rather than emailing or messaging them. You can glean so much more from a verbal conversation. For example you can get a sense if they are *fobbing you off* or they are being sincere.
- Avoid accusatory or confrontational language which might be challenging if you are a *Warrior*. As frustrated or angry as you may be, this tactic is never helpful.

- Be curious and start with something like "I was wondering if there's a problem why the payment has been overlooked? Is there a way you could settle it now or can we agree a payment date?"
- Remember an important point. You have a contract to deliver a service or product *in exchange* for payment unless you have agreed to offer your services for free. If you are a *People Pleaser*, I understand this will feel uncomfortable. However don't feel embarrassed to keep pressing. Know your worth!
- If you still have no luck, you can of course persist, but you also have a choice whether to accept that payment won't be forthcoming and to let it go, consider more formal action, or agree a payment plan if they are struggling to pay the full amount at once.

What about conversations where clients expect you to fulfil extra work that falls outside your agreed terms? How do you respectfully ask them to *back off* or say no without losing the contract?

If you are a copywriter for example, and your client asks if you would write an additional bio for a new team member for their website, although this surpasses the agreed number included in the fee.

Or perhaps your business is product based and your client asks if you can throw in a few more pieces for free once the order has been confirmed.

These are tricky conversations that require tact and tenacity and present a different set of challenges for both the *People Pleasers* and *Warriors*.

- Be clear and confident about setting boundaries. If you chose *not* to take the work on, try a response along the following lines. "This isn't something that is included in our contract or *Terms of Business*, but I would be more than happy to quote you for this". Or if it's product based, "As the order is now finalised, I can't add it on now but let me see what we can do for your next order". Play around with the words until it feels like your style. And practise saying it!
- Know your worth. If you *do* choose to take it at no additional cost, do so with the right intention and be clear (with yourself what that reason is). Don't agree to it because you have been guilt tripped or bullied into it, otherwise you will resent yourself, begrudge the client and won't deliver your best work.
- If you chose to take the work onboard because you'd like an ongoing relationship with this client, be happy with that choice knowing you have set a precedent that they might push you again. Alternatively agree to it as a one off but ensure they know that it's an exceptional situation and next time you will charge for it.

Managing Conflict with Business Partners

Hostility in relationships with business partners is not healthy for the business or your relationships. Fighting frequent battles is draining and prohibits decision making, business planning and progress for the company.

But it doesn't end here. When you are divided about the path ahead, this will also impact your relationships with your employees generating confusion and worries around loyalty. Who should they listen to and whose instructions should they follow?

So, what do you want? To be right or find a solution? The first step is to raise awareness of your trigger and theirs and what's fuelling your reaction to it because this will inform and energise the conversation.

- Invite curiosity rather than imposing your views and opinions. You won't win over and influence others with that strategy. Encourage others to do the same. Give all ideas an airing and an opportunity to be heard, don't shut them down but respectfully evaluate them.
- Press pause. You don't want to look back in anger with regret. Once said, those words are out there. They can't be *unsaid* or *unheard*. I think this quote sums it up. "Speak when you're angry and you will make the best speech you will ever regret!" (Ambrose Bierce)
- Have you ever seen the film Sliding Doors? I'm sure we've all experienced those moments or that split second when a conversation can go in one of two directions. These are the situations when you should have held back, but you *just* can't help yourself and something hurtful and toxic slipped out. The

chances of this happening increase when you're tired or stressed or your patience is waning.
- If you find the conversation (written or verbal) is going down a rabbit hole, it's totally acceptable to say: "Let's take a break "or "Can I come back to you on this?" In an hour, a day, a few days. Whatever is appropriate for the situation. Or "Let's pick this up again tomorrow once we've had a good night's sleep". That way you're giving yourself some breathing and thinking space, time to cool down, time for reflection and you're avoiding the opportunity of the tension and situation skyrocketing.
- Another sure way to push buttons and ensure no-one listens to the other is to raise your voice. And we all know what follows thereafter. Your colleague matches your tempo. And then you raise yours again. A bit like in a game of poker. *I'll see you and I'll raise you!* It's a disaster! This is where the *traffic light system* is very helpful. It's a myth that the louder you shout, the greater your chances of being heard! It will only incite further frustration or anger and will definitely not increase the odds of achieving a successful outcome! No matter how loud you shout!
- Don't over-talk. It will only encourage the same behaviour in return and shows no respect for others or their opinion.
- Don't repeat yourself. It's unlikely they will hear you better the second, third or fourth time!

Managing Compassionate Conversations

During the pandemic, I have been called upon many times for advice about managing these conversations more confidently. They require, empathy, understanding and sensitivity. These might have been centred around emotional and mental health or sharing news about the health of the business giving rise to redundancies.

These conversations aren't easy at the best of times, particularly if you are uncomfortable expressing emotion yourself. However this is the point. In these tough interactions, the focus should be on the other person and their experience, not your own discomfort.

Let's take the redundancy conversation.

This is likely to be one of the hardest leadership conversations you will ever need to master, and you are not alone. It is particularly heart-breaking when you share not only a professional relationship but also a personal one with your teams outside the workplace.

You may know their families, partners or even the names of their children and pets. This may bring up feelings of guilt and have an even more profound impact on you during and after the conversation.

You are likely to be faced with a host of challenging reactions and questions. Tears, anger, silence, 'Why me and not Annabelle?'.

- Prepare for pushback and keep the selection matrix in mind helping you stay focused, grounded and in control. It is often fear and panic that can throw us off kilter. Your team member will no doubt be

shocked at the finality of the news so allow time for the information to be processed. The silence may be agonising but avoid babbling to mask *your* anxiety and nerves.
- In those few minutes, put your emotions aside, no matter how dreadful you might be feeling. Don't draw out long explanations or share how difficult it has been for you. This will only frustrate and irritate them inciting further emotion.
- If HR are present at the *Consultancy and Final Meeting*, be clear who will lead the conversation and what each of your role will be, so the conversation is structured, fluid and your approach is unified. It might be useful, for example, for HR to explain the process, while your role is a supportive one.
- Consider what additional help you able to offer. For example, CV writing, strengths testing, interview technique or support packages. There are agencies that can help with this process so research these options before your meeting or ensure you revert back with this information soon afterwards.
- Be wary when working with external HR companies. While it is important to detach emotionally during these tough conversations, I heard a sad story where an employee was made redundant after ten years or more of service with a small family run business. The HR Business Partner who managed the process (and had never met the employee until that day), expressed how upset she was *to let her go*, which sparked further indignation and disbelief at her audacity and disrespect for the

longstanding and warm relationship she had enjoyed with her boss and colleagues.
- If you believe you might be in a position to rehire once the situation improves, share this but don't make false promises. Only make this commitment with integrity.
- There is no good time to deliver bad news. It might be useful however to factor in a few considerations regarding the timing of the conversation if your team member is working remotely. Are they a single parent looking after young children? Are they currently on sick leave and what will the impact of the news have on their health and emotional safety for them and those around at the time of the conversation?

What about those conversations around mental health or personal difficulties, when the conversation unexpectedly turns and your employee catches you off guard? These moments can be derailing and leaders and business owners I have discussed this with, have admitted to failing themselves and their team members during these delicate conversations. They feel disempowered to manage them competently leaving their team member feeling unsupported and themselves feeling inept.

This is a useful framework to support you through your compassionate conversations:

Listen:

Give them a good listening too! Listen without interrupting and pay attention too for what's not being said which might benefit from some further exploration. You know by now the power it can bring to restore calm and ease panic and tension.

Show empathy:

Acknowledge their struggles and pain. Statements such as "I can see this is distressing for you" or "I understand this is difficult" are good options.

Be present:

Show your presence by giving them your uninterrupted time and undivided attention.

Use the *3 T's:*

If the conversation becomes overwhelming, grab some *Tissues, Take a break* and in good old-fashioned British tradition during a crisis.... have a cup of *Tea*. The panacea for all emotional ailments and upset!

Invite curiosity:

They may find it hard to articulate their problems, particularly if they are upset or feel embarrassed if it's a financial concern. Ensure they are aware you are not there to judge but help. Or they may worry that they will lose control of their emotions. Gently scratch away the surface layer, getting to the essence by asking open questions that will help them to speak freely. For example, "I can see this is hard, but can you share what's going on?"

Support:

What guidance or help can you offer. If you're unsure about sick leave entitlement or anything related, check in with HR and then confirm back. Signpost them to you EAP (Employee Assistance Provider) if your business works with one for a host of counselling, therapy, and other services.

Use a M.A.P:

Manage your Mindset, be clear about the purpose of the conversation and what you hope to Achieve. Prepare yourself and notes if you have time.

Communicate with H.E.A.R.T:

Be humble, empathetic, authentic, respectful, and transparent.

Check in regularly:

Make a diary note to follow up and check in to see how they are. These small gestures will be remembered and appreciated.

Managing Cultural Obstacles

A few years ago, I was asked how to overcome cultural obstacles where it was considered disrespectful to speak up or challenge anyone in a senior position.

This becomes problematical when team members shut down when asked their opinion (if they disagree) with their boss, or they tow the party line and follow suit. Which means they never contribute original or noteworthy ideas.

A quiet conversation in a performance review would be the perfect opportunity to discuss this.

- If you understand your team member well enough, you will be aware of their motivators and drivers so draw on these and talk through why their job is important to them?
- Hone in on what they want to achieve in their role and their aspirations for growth. Ask how they imagine that will materialise if they don't contribute or speak up. Equally, ask them to visualise what will happen if they do.
- Explain all opinions are welcome and invited which supports the business culture and values and unlike their own culture, speaking up has positive consequences not negative ones.

Managing Mistakes

Mistakes will always happen. How you manage them will define you as a leader and how you will be remembered. It will dictate so much more than just the outcome of it but also your relationship moving forward, and the way mistakes are viewed as part of your culture.

I know several leaders who actively encourage failure or 'messing up' because that is one of the greatest learning and growth opportunities. And this approach demonstrates to your teams that it's ok to make a mistake, so they have no fear to own it, safe in the knowledge that there won't be consequences.

This also illustrates you are nurturing an open and transparent culture of psychological safety.

Yet these conversations can be challenging and problematic if mismanaged.

So, this is my advice and a useful strategy to approach the conversation to ensure the issue is addressed constructively and good relationships are maintained.

Three simple questions....

- *What just happened?* This is the chance to deconstruct the mistake and explore what went wrong and why. From their perspective and yours.
- *What are the implications of that?* A common problem is that your teams might not appreciate the impact of their mistakes which could impact collaborations, create delays on timelines, affecting other departments and the overall completion of projects or targets. Understanding this can help them be more conscious and cautious in the future.
- *What learnings can we take from that now?* Mistakes are always learning opportunities so discuss how your team member could prevent it next time and what that looks like. Be clear that they are clear.

Don't just ask *if* they have understood but *what* they have understood.

This story highlights a great example of a mistake managed kindly and compassionately. I know, because I was the one who made it!

When I worked in PR many years ago, we would often receive calls from journalists sniffing around for news stories.

Once the receptionists left for the day, everyone was expected to answer the phones. One evening, about 6:00 pm a journalist called. I picked up. Audaciously trying his luck, he asked when an announcement was being made relating to a time sensitive issue for one of our clients.

"Tomorrow at 9:00 am", I replied, proud to have been of help.

As I put the phone down, the realisation of what I had just done hit me! I had confirmed the existence of a confidential news story!

Heart pounding, I walked into my manager's office and shared the sorry events of the previous few minutes. I was met with a barrage of expletives and ushered unceremoniously out the room. The following sixty minutes passed in a haze as I nervously waited for my P45.

I was acutely aware of a hive of activity and people running up and down corridors!!

About an hour later, my chairman appeared. I held my breath waiting for the inevitable.

Instead, he sat me down and very gently talked me through the potential catastrophe I could have caused (as if I didn't already know!). But more importantly, he guided me through what I should have done and what to say in several different variations. I was so grateful for his kindness and patience. He was one of *the good guys*. Fortunately, he knew people in high places and managed to stop the leak being prematurely printed.

I learnt two important lessons that day. One to think before opening my mouth! The other, we are all human and will all make mistakes, however you can still manage them with kindness, patience and thought despite the severity or impact of them.

Managing Onboarding and New Recruits

If you're a small business owner or entrepreneur you might be considering your first hire or expanding your fast-growing empire. How much time and thought do you dedicate to the onboarding process, because this can be the reason the relationship falls apart before it has had the opportunity to flourish.

Whether you and your teams are partially or fully back in the office, here are a few helpful pointers to support you and them through their induction and to manage the early stage of your new relationship with success.

- Block time out to explain systems and process. If you need to allocate this to someone more technical or experienced, set this up and ask them to confirm once it has taken place.
- Be available as much as possible at least in the first few weeks to answer questions which may seem obvious to you because you know your business inside out, yet remember they aren't inside your head! Be patient.

- Don't throw them in the deep end until you feel they are ready. If they are the right fit for the business and your instincts were correct when you interviewed them, they will get there. Give them time.
- When you do start to increase their workload, give them autonomy but ensure they know you are available if they hit any bumps along the way and of course refer back to previous chapters for support!

Let's look now at the impact of the new team member on the rest of your team dynamics, the pitfalls if you hire the wrong person and the best way to introduce them into the business.

Perhaps, you've hired a new manager to reduce some of the load and to delegate tasks you no longer have time to deal with. This may have been a 'snap decision' hire without adequate thought and consideration whether this new team member will fit into the culture of your business or if their values are aligned with yours. It might have been a means of solving one problem (not enough time to do everything) yet just opening Pandora's box to another set of issues.

Where before your teams reported directly to you, now they would be reporting to someone who they begrudge, don't necessarily like or respect and whose communication style rubs them up the wrong way.

And with a lack of internal HR, some difficult conversations may fall by the wayside and resentment and hostility will bubble away under the surface towards both the new manager, who they consider is restricting contact with you, and to *you* for bringing in 'an outsider' and crushing the easy dynamics that you have enjoyed so far.

You may be less accessible and disconnected from your teams as you become focused on the bigger picture.

Flitting between meetings with investors, creatives, product designers, lawyers, accountants ... the list is exhaustive.

So, time for frustrating people problems amongst your teams might not take priority in the grand scheme of your expanding empire, however, you need to appreciate that this underlining friction could erupt at any moment.

The 'family environment' may still be a thing, yet suddenly the *'mother or father figure'* isn't as present.

So, what should you do?

- Brief the rest of your team *in advance* about the new manager's appointment. Be clear why you need this additional support and what their role will be. (Transparent communication!)
- Ensure your teams know you will still be available for them if not as visible. While you hope there won't be any roadblocks, encourage them to contact you whenever they need to. You have an open-door policy.
- Accept that the dynamics will change as the business grows. If issues crop up in their relationship with the new manager, don't assume it's their problem to manage, it's not. Make yourself accessible to smooth the pathway. It's your business so ultimately your responsibility to ensure it's a happy and harmonious place to work.
- Keep a close eye on morale and motivation. If you start to notice a slump in productivity or worse a

string of resignations, you will know your *snap hire* was a miscalculated mistake.

Managing Up

This is probably one of the most nerve-wracking of all conversations particularly if the feedback isn't solicited. It can be received defensively and at a high cost so a great deal rests on the quality of your relationship.

- Face the fear first. What are you afraid will happen if you bring the issue up? Are you concerned about the repercussions of it, if it will be rejected, a hostile response or how it will affect your relationship or your prospects within the business?
- Use a M.A.P and draw on all the mindset tools in chapter 6. This is so important to not just bring you confidence in yourself, but also clarity about the purpose of the conversation and the outcome you are hoping for. Prepare a list of anticipated responses from your boss and how to manage them. This will empower and support you in your delivery keeping you grounded and on track. As we now know, it is often the anticipation of the unknown that raises our anxiety. Being prepared is forearmed.
- Know your audience: Be mindful of the timing of the conversation. If you know your boss takes a yoga class at lunch time or is under immense pressure to meet a deadline, bear that in mind when you schedule the meeting. Be aware too of their style and mirror it. Don't waffle as this will probably frustrate.

- If nerves get the better of you, think of a time when you weren't afraid to speak up. This might be a conversation with a friend or colleague. Imagine yourself in that same conversation. Bottle that feeling.

Managing Team Conflict

This can be terrifying, overwhelming and confusing, particularly if you are a *Fresher* or *People Pleaser* who is repelled *by* and afraid *of* confrontation.

I have observed many new managers jump right in, with great gusto and enthusiasm yet lacking the judgement, skill, tools or experience to manage it competently.

Their ethos is *fix and solve* and then get the hell out of there as soon as possible! However this approach does not fly.

Because as you know, the sticky plaster method never unearths what's driving the conflict and the plaster will eventually peel off to reveal the wound once again, angrier, and now requiring a more substantial and intense solution. An *antibiotic* by way of a mediation for example.

I have witnessed too those leaders whose first response is to agree with one side over the other without embarking on a fact-finding mission and suddenly they have become entangled in the *conflict sandwich*, while the other team member kicks up a storm feeling justifiably unheard and resentful.

However just to be crystal clear, and to avoid the risk of becoming the bitter filling in the sandwich, we don't have to agree in order to understand and manage the issue.

I facilitated a mediation with a company a few years ago where one team member found it distracting to work in a noisy environment. As the office was open plan, this was challenging to control. They installed some dividers to reduce the noise levels yet there was one employee who had the loudest voice and very little self-awareness or EQ. He would often hover around his colleague's desk shouting across him or sharing banter with others.

Infuriated by this, his quieter colleague attempted to address it several times without success until one day, he lost his cool and nearly lost his job as a result of his unacceptable language and highly reactive response to his annoying colleague.

Unfortunately, the manager took sides without hearing the facts. While of course he had to address the outburst of the quieter employee, he never gave him the opportunity to share his narrative, leaving him aggrieved that he had been reprimanded and unheard and no closer to affecting a more productive working environment to concentrate.

Here the manager addressed the behaviour (not the symptom of it) and escalated the problem by not giving one employee a voice and the right to reply while appearing to side with his colleague.

When we are embroiled in a conflict, we actively seek confirmation from others that we are right. And this is what your team members will attempt to do too. But don't fall into this trap. What you can offer instead is your ear and empathy using the *traffic light system* to diffuse both sides first before moving the conversation forward.

Here are two effective tools we use in mediation to follow through with. The first is the **B.I.N**. method and looks at the behaviours of both team members.

1. Acknowledge the unwelcome **Behaviour**: For example, one may feel aggrieved that his colleague shuts him down in meetings by dismissing his ideas and opinions.
2. Explore the **Impact** of the behaviour: He feels ignored, belittled, humiliated and unvalued.
3. What does he **Need** instead: Respect and acknowledgement that his colleague listens to his views, asks for his input and gives his ideas the chance to be discussed?

The other technique is: *What I would like? What I can offer in return?*

This method is useful when you hit a roadblock or impasse. To begin, it's important to look for commonality. Both team member may be seeking the opportunity to have their narrative heard and their perspective acknowledged which means they want their opinion or value respected.

And here's where the mutuality comes in. They **both** seek respect. So, ask them individually what respectful communication looks like.

And then follow up with these two additional questions for them need to consider.

What they would each like (*from the other party*)

The answer to this might be for example... 'I'd like x to stop raising his / her voice at me in meetings'.

And then I ask the *same* person:

What can they offer (*to the other party*)?

The response to this might be... "In return, I will listen without constantly interrupting".

This whole process is then repeated with the other party.

With this tool, both colleagues have the opportunity for mutual respect and their unmet need is also being satisfied. Their valued value is being acknowledged.

So, if you find yourself caught between a rock and a hard place and don't know how to help colleagues see each other's perspective, try this approach which will hopefully show them what it's like to wear a different pair of shoes!

Finally, if you do find yourself heading down a rabbit hole, remember it's better to ask for support from other colleagues, an experienced friend, or your own boss rather than botching it up only to escalate the conflict to a crisis!

Managing Strong Personalities:

We've all faced one at some time, I'm sure. Those big, intimidating personalities who we have to work with. Yet as you will now know, behind every behaviour is a message.

Let's look at this example.

You've just been given the dream promotion managing a new division. Yet with the new role comes a new and very challenging personality who you have been asked to collaborate with. It is an understatement to say your management and communication style clash!

It's more like Clash of the Titans!

In your first meeting, a touch of *Warrior* emerges in both of you as you throw your weight, ego and ideas around the table. It's not pretty, productive, or helpful. Neither of you are listening to each other, but ironically, you both want to be heard.

What do you do?

- Stop trying to compete!
- Try and understand what is sitting underneath their behaviours (and yours). Perhaps you are both feeling threatened, afraid, or insecure that your ideas won't be as good as your colleague's. Are you seeking one-upmanship or recognition from your boss?
- Find common ground. Ultimately you both want to be respected, heard, and acknowledged.
- Listen to each other. You know this is your silver bullet. Use the *traffic light system*.
- Make the conversation inclusive and about you both. Ask how you can collaborate.

It will take time and effort to build trust and rapport, but this is a good time to lay the foundations and define the perimeters of your new relationship.

Micro-managing

Micro-managing is an unhelpful leadership style and has become more prevalent since Covid-19 as many businesses have adopted a hybrid workplace. Yet it is unwelcome, damaging and toxic.

To begin, I would invite some self-reflection.

What is driving your incessant need to watch your teams like a hawk? A fear of missed deadlines or targets which reflects badly on you?

Or is this leadership style based on a mistrust that your employees won't manage their task competently which means you will spend more time and energy rectifying it?

Or is your *supervisory behaviour* driven by your desire for perfectionism that their work will be sub-standard?

In order to prevent this unhelpful style, I would encourage some reflective practice to recognize why you are micro-managing, because once this is understood and acknowledged, you are better placed to change your own behaviours. Here are some thoughts.

- Are the deadlines you set realistic and have you checked that your team member is comfortable and confident to meet them? If this a frequent occurrence, it's not unreasonable to be troubled the same will happen this time. However, as is the case in many behavioral issues, it is better to address the cause and not the symptom and to discuss the obstacles impeding the success and how to overcome them at the time when the task is set.
- Do you believe your team member is adequately supported to complete the assignment? While it is vitally important to give them autonomy and allow them to make mistakes in order to grow, the purpose is not to set them up for failure. It is a balance. Ensure you provide all the necessary support and back up particularly if they are new to the business.
- Manage expectations. Be as specific as possible about what you require from your team member in terms of timings, delivery, behaviours, presentation, content or anything that is important to meet the standards you are expecting. In my experience, misalignment of values often crops up as a driver in micro-managing behaviours because you and your

team member might be on completely different pages.

The Return to Office Conversation

Well, this has certainly been a bone of contention globally. While some businesses and industries require their employees to be in the workplace full time because of the nature of the work, others have had no choice but to adopt an agile and flexible arrangement.

Many employees have expressed that they miss the connection, rapport, team building opportunities, community spirit and creativity that working together inspires, others attest to working far more productively and efficiently in the quiet of their own environment, saving time and money on commuting.

The problem arises though around fairness and consistency with *working from home* days vs *in office* days. What may appear fair to you, might seem totally unfair to your team. Do you make exceptions? If so, is this rolled out across the board? Do you have a policy in place for all managers to follow when they are faced with these challenging requests?

My experience is that the businesses who have carefully considered and explored their new agile working arrangements based on their business model, the business requirements and those of their employees, are the ones who will have less resistance and challenge implementing them.

While you will never, please everyone, if you are met with resistance, it's important to share your criteria and the *why* behind your decisions.

So here we conclude the final chapter.

I would like to offer you one final parting piece of advice...

If you hit a roadblock in your difficult conversations, refer to your M.A.P, ask for directions by being C.U.R.I.O.U.S and always communicate with H.E.A.R.T!

EPILOGUE

So, this is the end of our journey together.

My wish is that this book has given you knowledge to prevent and circumnavigate conflict swiftly, trust that no conversation will ever be an impossible feat to overcome and faith in your abilities to manage it proficiently, confidently and courageously.

I hope you have not only enjoyed reading it but now feel equipped and ready to embrace your difficult conversations with more panache and poise. It will take time and practise to master them, but master them you will!

As each conversation becomes less problematic and effortless to navigate, you will notice an improvement in your relationships too. Your working day will be more productive as you spend less time fretting over those challenging interactions and more time focusing on the business of business.

Life will be less stressful, more relaxed and so much easier! Who knows, the lessons learnt may even benefit your relationships outside the workplace too! Good luck! *And Breathe...*

ABOUT THE AUTHOR

Nicole is a Communication and Conflict Expert, empowering Leaders and Business Owners to minimise conflict through more effective communication. She supports her clients to successfully navigate difficult conversations with confidence and finesse to create harmonious and thriving workplaces.

As a Consultant, Coach, Trainer and accredited Workplace Mediator, she has an interest in the psychology of conflict combined with extensive experience in communications following a background in PR.

She is author of many published articles on communication and workplace conflict in the following publications: Thrive Global, SME Magazine, HR Magazine and is a senior guest contributor to BRAINZ Magazine.

She was featured in COACH Magazine in 2020 and has contributed to several articles in Metro (online), Psychologies Magazine and numerous other work-life publications. She's a regular podcast guest discussing conflict and communication issues in the workplace.

Nicole was voted Communication and Conflict Consultant of the Year in the Greater London Enterprise Awards 2022. In 2021 she was included in the *Brainz 500 Global List* as one of 500 influential leaders and in 2020 she was a shortlisted finalist in the UK National Mediation Awards.

Nicole lives in London with her husband Julian. She is proud to have 3 sons, 3 step-children, 4 grandchildren and 2 dogs!

Get in touch ...

While I have included as much as I can into this book, please contact me if you would like further support or to discuss how to work with me.

Visit my website: www.nicoleposner.com
Email me on: nicole@posner.london

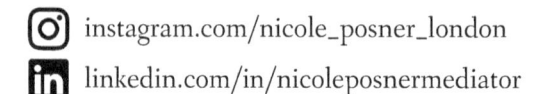

instagram.com/nicole_posner_london
linkedin.com/in/nicoleposnermediator

CPSIA information can be obtained
at www.ICGtesting.com
Printed in the USA
BVHW091135300922
648382BV00021B/1319/J